THE ENGLISH COCKER SPANIEL

Tammy Gagne

The English Cocker Spaniel
 Project Team
Editor: Adam Taliercio
Copy Editor: Joann Woy
Indexer: Elizabeth Walker
Designer: Stephanie Krautheim
Series Design: Stephanie Krautheim and Mada Design
Series Originator: Dominique De Vito

T.F.H. Publications
President/CEO: Glen S. Axelrod
Executive Vice President: Mark E. Johnson
Publisher: Christopher T. Reggio
Production Manager: Kathy Bontz

T.F.H. Publications, Inc.
One TFH Plaza
Third and Union Avenues
Neptune City, NJ 07753

Printed and bound in China

08 09 10 11 12   1 3 5 7 9 8 6 4 2

Library of Congress Cataloging-in-Publication Data

Gagne, Tammy.
  The English cocker spaniel / Tammy Gagne.
    p. cm.
  Includes index.
  ISBN 978-0-7938-3685-7 (alk. paper)
  1. English cocker spaniel. I. Title.
  SF429.E47G34 2008
  636.752'4--dc22
                                                    2008024532

This book has been published with the intent to provide accurate and authoritative information in regard to the
subject matter within. While every reasonable precaution has been taken in preparation of this book, the author
and publisher expressly disclaim responsibility for any errors, omissions, or adverse effects arising from the use or
application of the information contained herein. The techniques and suggestions are used at the reader's discretion
and are not to be considered a substitute for veterinary care. If you suspect a medical problem consult your
veterinarian.

The Leader In Responsible Animal Care For Over 50 Years!®
www.tfh.com

TABLE OF CONTENTS

1

HISTORY

of the English Cocker Spaniel

One of the oldest dog breeds of all time, the English Cocker Spaniel has a magnificent history that reads a bit like a fairy tale. Within this exciting story there lies the legend of a talented hunter, a breed-changing voyage across an ocean, and the promise of unconditional love for those who care for him. His journey is not without conflict, of course. The handsome hero faces many obstacles along the way, but in the end, as in all good fairy tales, he triumphs over his challenges and becomes a source of joy, companionship, and pride to all around him.

ENGLISH COCKER SPANIEL OR AMERICAN COCKER SPANIEL?

Owners in the United Kingdom (UK) generically refer to this familiar breed as the Cocker Spaniel. Occasionally, if owners are also discussing the breed's closely related cousin, the American Cocker Spaniel, they may instead use the term English Cocker Spaniel for the sake of clarity. When neither type is specified, however, one can safely assume that the breed in question is indeed the English Cocker.

In the United States, however, when people mention a Cocker Spaniel, chances are very good that it is the American Cocker to whom they are referring. In the UK and many other areas of the world, this dog is considered the *American* Cocker Spaniel, though. So what is the difference? Which dog is the true Cocker Spaniel? The answers to these questions may depend largely upon whom you ask.

Although physical differences certainly exist between the two breeds now, these two dogs not only share a nearly identical history, but also many of the same characteristics and needs in terms of care. For this reason, one may assume that the advice within this guide pertains to both the English and American Cocker Spaniels, except where otherwise specified.

FROM SPAIN TO ENGLAND

All spaniels can be traced to their original country of Spain, where they were

The lineage of the English Cocker Spaniel traces back to Spain, where the breed was used as hunting dogs.

Pardon My French

A British historian by the name of Colonel David Hancock offered two other possible origins for the word "spaniel." He suggested that it may have derived from the French word *espanir*, which means "to crouch"—the breed's conventional hunting posture. Hancock also drew attention to the Italian word *spaniare*, which means "to get out of a trap or net"—the method of game hunting Cocker Spaniel owners utilized prior to the introduction of firearms.

predominantly used to hunt game. The word "spaniel" is most likely derived from the French phrase "*chiens de l' Espagnol*," which means "dog of Spain." Many believe the breed was introduced to England as early as the time of Caesar's invasion (around 55 BCE).

Utilized as hunting dogs on the estates of wealthy British citizens, spaniels quickly gained prestige as bird dogs with a discerning talent for hunting in forests, pointing (directing their masters to game) in high brush, and flushing birds out of thickets. They were also known for their impressive retrieving skills.

Prior to the invention of firearms, hunting dogs worked in conjunction with birds of prey—primarily hawks and falcons. (The presence of a predator bird flying overhead would ensure that the game remained earthbound.) The spaniel's job was to track and flush game birds so that his owner could catch them with a net. Once the shotgun was introduced, however, predator birds were

no longer necessary, and the spaniel became the solitary cohort of the 17th century game hunter.

A Family of Spaniels

The British continued to breed and develop spaniels to suit a variety of purposes. By the early 19th century, the dogs best suited for hunting pheasant, grouse, and woodcock were aptly delineated "cocking" or "cocker spaniels." Although so-called "springing spaniels" possessed a similar talent for hunting, the Cocker Spaniel (perhaps due to his more maneuverable size) worked faster, was more adept at scenting, and made his way through short, dense terrain much more easily than the dog now known as the Springer Spaniel. The Cocker was also considerably more proficient at retrieving game from the water.

During this pivotal period, Springer Spaniels, Sussex Spaniels, and Cocker Spaniels were all born within the same litters. Size alone set the designations: the largest puppies were classified Springers, the medium dogs were dubbed Sussex Spaniels, and the smallest puppies were considered Cockers. When bench shows (early versions of contemporary dog shows) were first held in England, this size-based classification system proved to be problematic. A dog who was originally entered as a Cocker Spaniel was often categorized as a Springer the very next year due to his continued growth.

Excelling at Work

In addition to the dogs' obvious hunting abilities, these ancestors to our modern-day English Cockers also exhibited a clear love for their work. While in the fields doing what they did best, their tails were noted to be in constant motion, punctuating the

One Faithful Canine

Would you believe that a Cocker Spaniel might have played a role in England's separation from the Catholic Church? It has been rumored that when Henry VIII was seeking a divorce from Catherine of Aragon, he sent a man by the name of Lord Wiltshire to Rome on his behalf to obtain the permission of Pope Clement VII. A devoted dog owner, Lord Wiltshire brought his favorite spaniel along for the trip. When the lord knelt to ceremonially kiss the pontiff's feet, the pope moved unexpectedly. This startled the dog who perceived the action as a threat to his beloved owner and bit the pope at once on the toe. Although we may never know if the pope indeed held a grudge, the divorce was ultimately denied, and a short time later Henry VIII severed his relations with the Catholic Church, beginning the formation of the Church of England.

The ancestors of the modern English Cocker Spaniel were excellent hunters with unyielding dedication to their work.

dogs' unyielding dedication to their task with a passionate display of elation and fulfillment.

By 1850, Cocker Spaniel breeders began keeping track of their dogs' pedigrees, although it was still some time before pen and paper were used to record this information—for many years it was merely committed to memory. When the Kennel Club (KC) of England was formed in 1873, members attempted to retroactively document Cocker litters whelped as far back as 1859 for the organization's first stud books. The Cocker would not be given official status in these registers, however, for nearly another 20 years.

Classifying Spaniels

Since there were still many different types of spaniels in England during this period, classifications between the different spaniel breeds also needed to be made at this time. Most cocking dogs of this era generally weighed between 14 and 20 pounds (6.3 and 9 kg), so the decision was made to officially categorize all spaniels weighing less than 25 pounds (11.3 kg) as Cocker Spaniels. Some of these dogs, like those known previously as Welsh (or Devonshire) Spaniels, were initially labeled Cocker Spaniels but were ultimately reclassified as Welsh Springer Spaniels in 1903 as part of the English Springer Spaniel registry.

Formal Recognition

The first official credit of the Cocker Spaniel came in 1892, when the breed was finally given status in the KC's Stud Book. In 1901, the 25-pound (11.3-kg) weight restriction was removed as a breed trait. The American Kennel Club (AKC) has recognized the breed since the 1880s, when Cocker Spaniels began to be exhibited in the US.

The Cocker Spaniel Club (CSC), the official parent club of the breed, was formed in England over a century ago. One of the club's primary goals was to create a breed standard, a detailed description of the Cocker Spaniel for breeders and judges alike. At this time, the club's membership totaled just 35. The current membership is well over 1,500 and includes English Cocker Spaniel fanciers from 48 nations. Along with the number of CSC members, the number of registered English Cockers also grew dramatically around this time—from 8,000 dogs in 1935 to 25,000 in just a single decade. The current number falls short of this remarkable pinnacle, but present-day registrations for this popular breed still top 12,000.

ACROSS THE ATLANTIC

Exported from Britain to the US and Canada in the 1870s, Cocker Spaniels were headed for several changes as this lovable new breed penetrated North America. Perhaps the most significant of these was the dog's enormous popularity in the show ring. Although the breed had always enjoyed a favorable reception from its British fanciers, the Cocker's entrance into America marked the beginning of organized conformation shows on both sides of the Atlantic. The Cocker Spaniel was finally being recognized just as much for his beauty and charisma as for his proven abilities in the field.

The Separation of English and American Cockers

With its new larger audience, the Cocker Spaniel also underwent more tangible transformations, particularly during the 1920s and '30s. While British kennels continued the well-established goal of producing quality gundogs, many fanciers in the US began breeding more for aesthetic purposes than for hunting ability. This is where the English and American Cocker Spaniel breeds truly began to go their separate ways.

The new American Cocker Spaniels were bred to be slightly smaller than their English counterparts. Most were approximately two inches shorter at the withers with a smaller head and muzzle and a more dramatic down-slope of the top line. American Cockers also had longer, silkier hair, as well as a denser coat.

Although an overwhelming number of dog lovers in the US fell in love with this more glamorous Cocker Spaniel, a substantial number still preferred the traditional style of the breed, which focused instead on function. English Cockers offered definite advantages to their owners—including better endurance and higher visibility in the field, likely due to the dog's slightly larger size and additional weight. The English Cocker's larger muzzle also allowed him to carry bigger game birds than his American counterpart. Of course, owners of American Cockers still insist that their dogs' ability to fit into smaller spaces is likewise an advantage in the field. Whichever variation an owner preferred, though, one thing was certain: the English and American Cockers were becoming two separate—yet similar—breeds.

In 1935, E. Shippen Willing formed the English Cocker Spaniel Club of America, an organization devoted to the preservation of the English Cocker. The club's first show was held that same year at Willing's estate near Bryn Mawr, Pennsylvania, and included 40 dogs—an impressive number for the time. Thanks to the dedicated work of Mrs. Geraldine R. Dodge, the club's then-president, the breed lines of English and American Cockers were painstakingly

The English Cocker was first recognized by the AKC in 1946.

Kennel Club History

After dogfighting was outlawed in the 1830s and '40s, dog shows developed as a way for owners to display their dogs in a more positive way. The first organized event of this kind occurred in Great Britain in 1859; the first North American show was held in Quebec, Canada, in 1867. With no breed standards as guidelines, however, judging the dogs was problematic— the rules seemed to be different at each show. There were also no standards for obedience within the ring, so mayhem frequently ensued.

The Kennel Club was founded in 1873 to create basic rules for the show ring. The establishment of the American Kennel Club followed in 1884, and then the Canadian Kennel Club in 1888. Today, kennel clubs are nonprofit organizations whose members work together to create and uphold standards for all dog-related issues, including the registration and showing of purebred dogs. Many such clubs exist in countries throughout the world, but the KC and the AKC remain two of the most prominent and influential.

separated over the next decade, paving the way for the English Cocker Spaniel to be recognized officially as a breed of its own by the AKC in 1946. In the UK, American Cockers were granted status as a separate breed by the KC in 1968. Although the two breeds would always remain connected through their mutual history and similar appearance, the lines would no longer be interbred.

As American owners of English Cockers worked to maintain their dogs' identity, popularity of the breed's American cousin grew even more dramatically. The American Cocker Spaniel became the AKC's number one breed in 1936—and remained at or near the top for more than half a century. Although no longer the headliner of the AKC's most popular breeds list, the American Cocker is still greatly adored by the American public. The English Cocker also maintains an intensely loyal following in the US, although it has never been among the most commonly registered breeds with the AKC.

THE PRICE OF FAME

Like many other fashionable breeds, the American Cocker Spaniel experienced a surge of popularity so intense that it eventually became the dog's biggest downfall. Everybody wanted a Cocker, and unprincipled breeders took full advantage of what they saw as a lucrative business opportunity. Reckless breeding practices won out over maintaining the very qualities that made the

Elizabeth Barrett Browning's cherished English Cocker Spaniel, Flush, was immortalized in writing twice—first by the 19th century poet herself in a poem bearing the dog's name and again in 1931 by author Virginia Woolf in an imaginative biography (also aptly named *Flush*) about the Cocker Spaniel's adventures as Barrett Browning's pet.

dog so well liked in the first place.

Through these dark years, puppy mills and backyard breeders brought a new connotation to the American Cocker breed—one of surly temperament and poor health, problems never before seen in this breed. (Since the English Cocker never reached the same level of popularity in the US as the American Cocker Spaniel, it was not subjected to the same ruthless mass-breeding practices. Consequently, it was also not beset with the same problems relating to health and temperament.)

Thanks to the hard work and dedication of responsible breeders, however, the damage caused to the American Cocker Spaniel breed was fortunately not irreparable. Although puppy mills are still one of the greatest threats to all purebred dogs, hobby breeders—the moral fiber of the Cocker Spaniel community—have succeeded in bringing the breed back to its most important original purpose—that of a loving and stable companion.

HAVEN'T I SEEN YOU SOMEWHERE BEFORE?

In addition to being revered by a passionate mainstream public, English Cocker Spaniels have also been immortalized in history through the writings of such literary greats as Chaucer, Shakespeare, and Elizabeth Barrett Browning. More contemporary fanciers of the breed include the Queen of England herself. Her Majesty breeds and trains English Cockers (along with Labradors) at Sandringham.

Even US presidents have caught Cocker fever: Rutherford B. Hayes owned a Cocker Spaniel named Dot; Shannon was the name of John F. Kennedy's English Cocker; and who could forget Richard Nixon's legendary Cocker, Checkers? (Nixon made Checkers famous with a speech now often referred to by the dog's name alone.)

In 1955, the Cocker Spaniel made his (or her, as the case may be) big-screen debut in Walt Disney's animated feature *Lady and the Tramp*. In this romantic adventure, the title characters—a purebred Cocker Spaniel named Lady and a fun-loving mongrel—try to outrun the dogcatcher, romp through wet cement, and share an unforgettable candlelight dinner of spaghetti and meatballs. The film stole America's heart, once again catapulting the Cocker to star status, this time more literally.

Around the same time, a major US company decided to include the Cocker Spaniel in a national advertising campaign. Created by artist Joyce Ballantyne Brand, *Little Miss Coppertone* and her mischievous Cocker Spaniel, who was pulling down the young girl's bathing suit, graced billboards from San Francisco to Manhattan. It may even be said that a real, live Cocker launched the career of superstar Jodie Foster when, at the age of three, she appeared as the tow-headed, bare-bottomed child in the television version of the now famous ad.

The modern English Cocker Spaniel still possesses that same playful attitude captured in Brand's now collectible illustration. The breed's devotion to play is in fact the only thing that might possibly equal the dogs' devotion to their owners. It is, in my opinion, the breed's most endearing feature—until you have gotten down on your hands and knees to play with your dog at his insistence, you have not truly experienced the essence of what it means to own an English Cocker Spaniel.

Hey Bird Dog!

Looking for a song about a Cocker? In 1958, the Everly Brothers recorded a song called "Bird Dog", which is particularly special to me, as my very first Cocker Spaniel was named Johnny, the name mentioned over and over again in the lyrics.

The English Cocker Spaniel of today is known for his playful and intelligent nature.

CHARACTERISTICS

of the English Cocker Spaniel

W hat makes an English Cocker an English Cocker? Is it the long ears? Or maybe the feathered legs? Perhaps it's those powerful eyes that make your heart melt the minute you see them. If you had to choose one quality that makes this breed stand out from the rest, you would be hard pressed to pinpoint a single characteristic that makes the English Cocker Spaniel so unique. Indeed, it is the combination of all the breed's traits—both physical and otherwise—that makes this magnificent dog the object of so much affection.

Certainly, the English Cocker Spaniel's endearing looks are part of his huge appeal. Whether coifed to perfection in a full coat for show or clipped shorter for a more playful appearance, the English Cocker is striking from head to toe. To many, he is the quintessential dog: beautiful, bright, and hardworking.

A member of the sporting group, the English Cocker has a sturdy but compact body. Many people are amazed by how muscular English Cockers can be (and most only find out when cuddling with one). The American Kennel Club (AKC) standard for the breed states that it is compact, and it truly is. The English Cocker almost always has the energy for one more lap around the block, but he is also reasonably portable—light enough to be carried on the rare occasion that he runs out of gas halfway home, or just because you feel like picking him up for a quick hug.

SIZE AND STATURE

An ideal adult male should stand 16 to 17 inches (40.6 to 43.2 cm) at the withers. For females, this measurement should be 15 to 16 inches (38.1 to 40.6 cm). The weight range for males is 28 to 34 pounds (12.7 to 15.4 kg) and 26 to 32 pounds (11.8 to 14.5 kg) for females. Seen in profile, the English Cocker Spaniel's silhouette is instantly recognizable. The measurement from the withers to the ground should be approximately the same as that from the withers to the root of the dog's tail.

The English Cocker has a sturdy and muscular but compact body.

HEAD

The head is considered by many to be the breed's most endearing feature. With his merry nature, intelligent expression, and long, flowing ears, the English Cocker is instantly recognized by this single body part. The eyes are dark brown. The dog's nose—with the well-developed nostrils indicative of a sporting dog—should balance the square muzzle. The jaw is strong, with teeth arranged in a complete scissors bite.

BODY AND TAIL

Although not overly long, the English Cocker Spaniel's muscular neck should enable his nose to comfortably reach the ground. The dog's topline slopes slightly toward the quarters, accentuating that famous stance. The chest is deep and well developed, and the ribs are well sprung.

Tradition calls for a docked tail that should be neither too long nor too short. Although never held in a timid position, the tail also shouldn't be carried straight up. It should be carried on a plane no higher than the level of the animal's back. When the dog is moving, the tail embodies the breed's nature of general exuberance.

The English Cocker Spaniel's front legs are well boned and straight. They should be short enough for concentrated power, but not so short as to interfere with performance. The hindquarters should also be wide, well-rounded, and muscular—with a good bend of stifle. This allows for plenty of drive. Feet should be firm and thickly padded—"catlike," as the breed standard puts it.

Why Do English Cockers Have Docked Tails?

Tail docking is a very old custom involving the removal of between one-half and two-thirds of a dog's tail. The original purpose of docking an English Cocker Spaniel's tail was to prevent the dog from becoming wounded or overrun with burrs while hunting in heavy brush. Obviously, only a small number of present-day pet English Cockers face this kind of threat, so the contemporary practice of tail docking has become a rather controversial topic in certain circles. Is it really necessary? The answer isn't as clear as one may think.

Opponents of docking insist that it is a cruel practice done purely for superficial, cosmetic reasons. They stress such possible risks as infection, hemorrhaging, and even meningitis. For these reasons, some breeders have long been skipping this tradition, and opting instead to celebrate the beauty of a natural, full English Cocker Spaniel tail by allowing it to remain intact.

Those who support docking explain that it still serves some

American Cockers

The visual differences between the English Cocker Spaniel and his American cousin are noticed immediately when looking at both dogs' heads. The American Cocker has a distinctly domed skull, a shorter muzzle, and larger, more prominent eyes with more clearly defined eyebrows. The American Cocker also has a more profuse coat than the English Cocker Spaniel. The English Cocker coat is flat and silky in texture. It is never wiry, wavy, or curly. While the American Cocker Spaniel's coat is said to be feathered, many breeders of English Cockers instead refer to their dogs' fur as being fringed. This more sculpted coat emphasizes the true shape of the body. As one English Cocker Spaniel breeder states, "The American Cocker has a coat that can hide a lot of faults."

important purposes. English Cockers are born with rather sizeable tails; some breeders charge that they are so large, in fact, that the dogs can actually hurt themselves by hitting these disproportionate appendages against themselves or other objects. They also claim that fecal matter and dirt tend to congregate around a bushier tail, and that docking is in this way also a matter of better hygiene.

Until very recently, most breeders have docked tails when their litters were just a few days old. At this extremely young age, the nerves within a dog's tail are not yet fully developed, so the puppies are considerably less vulnerable to pain from the procedure. As of 2007, however, the procedure became illegal in England, Scotland, and Wales. An exemption for working dogs does exist in England and Wales, but owners who utilize this exemption still may not be able to show their animals in conformation. There is no exemption in Scotland. Legislation regarding docking is still in its early stages in Northern Ireland. For detailed advice on following this new legislation, please visit the KC website at www. thekennelclub.org.uk. (Tail docking is still legal in the US.)

Many people believe that tail docking, like ear cropping for other dog breeds, will be made illegal in most countries at some point in the future. Presently, English Cockers with full tails are not

Some breeders carry on the tradition of docking the English Cocker's tail, but the practice has become less popular with time.

eligible to participate in AKC conformation events, but if similar legislation passes in the US, this disqualification will become a thing of the past, as it has in the UK. If you compare the tails of younger English Cockers today to those dogs docked in the past, you will see that US breeders are already leaving more and more length—5 inches (12.7 cm) or more in some cases, as opposed to just barely 3 inches (7.6 cm), the average length just a decade or so ago. Leaving the tail fully intact may indeed be a natural progression of this trend.

Baby's Got Blue Eyes

Most English Cocker Spaniels are born with striking blue eyes. This distinctive feature will change gradually over the first year, usually into a shade of dark brown by adulthood.

COAT

In the show ring, the English Cocker coat is preferred to be silky and flat. While a wavy coat is considered acceptable, curly dogs are severely penalized. Many times a curly coat is merely the result of insufficient brushing during the blow-drying process or allowing a dog to air-dry after a bath. If you have no plans for showing your dog, however, a curly coat will do little to detract from an attractive appearance; moreover, depending on your personal tastes, it may even add to it.

COLORS—BUFF AND BEYOND

My first Cocker was buff (golden) in color, and I can honestly say without prejudice (well, almost) that he was one of the most handsome dogs I have ever seen. I have also been blessed to know many other gorgeous buff dogs over the years—each with a unique shade of blond fur. I'm sure you have also seen countless dogs in this traditional English Cocker color. While none can deny the appeal of this classic look, many people new to the breed are surprised to learn just how many other colors and combinations of colors English Cockers can actually be.

Black and ASCOB

The flip side of buff, black is also a relatively common color for dogs of this breed. Just as some people prefer the lighter golden tones, others find solid black English Cockers to be the epitome of beauty and grace. All solid colors except for black—which include liver, red, and buff—are categorized as ASCOB, an acronym for "Any Solid Color Other than Black."

Parti-Colored

In addition to the sensational solids, English Cockers of combined colors (parti-colored dogs) are also available. These slightly lesser known varieties can be equally as breathtaking as their monochromatic cousins. Dogs of various colors and combinations can be born not only to the same parents, but also within the very same litters. The variety of puppies born in a particular litter depends on the lineage of the parents. Frequently, breeders strive to produce a specific variety of English Cockers, but even in these cases, no guarantees exist for what kind of an assortment they will ultimately get.

Merle

In addition to the mainstream parti-colored varieties, you may find other, even more unusual combinations of colors and markings. One such rare variety is the merle coat pattern. Due to a special gene that essentially dilutes the colors of certain hairs within the coat, these dogs take on a most unique look. In so-called "blue merles," the dog's black and diluted black (or silver) hairs take on a brilliant blue sheen. The merle pattern can also appear in a variety of other colors. Merle-patterned dogs might have brown eyes, blue eyes, or in some instances, one of each. Since they are so rare,

English Cockers are available in a wide variety of colors.

Engllish Cocker Spaniel Colors

Solid Colors

- Black
- Liver with brown pigmentation
- Red with black pigmentation
- Red with brown pigmentation (unusual)
- Golden with black pigmentation
- Golden with brown pigmentation (unusual)

Rare But Not Yet Universally Recognized Colors

- Sable (sometimes classified as parti-colored for show purposes)
- Silver-ash (a dilute black)
- White with black/brown pigmentation

Tan Mask & Trim

- Black and tan
- Liver and tan (sometimes called chocolate and tan)
- Red/golden and tan (not usually visible to the eye)
- Silver-ash and tan (in dilute variant)

Roan Markings

- Blue roan
- Liver roan (sometimes called chocolate roan)
- Orange roan (with black pigmentation)
- Orange roan (with brown pigmentation)
- Lemon roan (with black pigmentation)
- Lemon roan (with light brown pigmentation, most recessive of all roans)

Parti-Color and White (Ticked)

- Black and white (ticked with flecks of black)
- Liver and white (ticked with flecks of brown)
- Orange and white (ticked with flecks of orange, with black pigmentation)
- Orange and white (ticked with flecks of orange, with brown pigmentation)
- Lemon and white (ticked with flecks of lemon, with black pigmentation)
- Lemon and white (ticked with flecks of lemon, with brown pigmentation)

Note: All of the ticked pattern colors may carry a tan mask and trim if both parents carry the separate gene for this marking.

Parti-Color and White

- Black and white (skin of nonpigmented white area is pink)
- Liver and white (always with brown pigmentation)
- Orange and white (with black pigmentation)
- Orange and white (with brown pigmentation)
- Lemon and white (ticked with flecks of lemon, with black pigmentation)
- Lemon and white (ticked with flecks of lemon, with brown pigmentation)

Note: All of the "and white" colors may have a tan mask and trim if both of the parents carry the separate gene for this trait.

White English Cockers are rarely born. In fact, they are usually black and whites, orange and whites, or lemon and whites with just a few flecks of marking. White spaniels are thought to be more prone to deafness than those with more pigmentation, and are not generally encouraged in the breed as a result.

(Courtesy of the Cocker Spaniel Club)

merle-patterned dogs are always in high demand.

While breeders *can* safely use merles in their breeding programs, it is vitally important that a merle is never bred to another merle. Mating two merle dogs (of any breed) usually results in a litter of blind, deaf, or so severely malformed puppies that they are either stillborn or die soon after birth.

Roan

Another rare and stunning coat variation is the roan pattern. Unlike the merle pattern, which is distinctive at birth, a roan appearance emerges over time. In a parti-colored dog, the predominant color progressively develops throughout the remainder of the coat. Similar to a blue merle, a blue roan is actually mostly black. The dog's white fur becomes peppered with this prevailing color, causing the remarkable illusion of being blue. Unlike dogs with heavy ticking (a mixture of color resulting from spots dispersed throughout the coat), English Cockers with a roan pattern have roan ancestors within their pedigrees.

The English Cocker has a sweet temperament that makes him a suitable addition to virtually any family able and willing to care for him.

Sable

A third uniquely stunning variety is the sable English Cocker Spaniel. Like the merles and the roans, sable dogs take on their extraordinary appearance from a mixture of differently colored hairs. In this case it is an interlacing of black hairs throughout a lighter background color that usually results in a dazzling brown that can range from golden to mahogany. Although some other breeds—the Collie and Sheltie, for instance—also come in sable varieties, the sable English Cocker is theorized to be unique in that the hairs are not tipped or banded in black, but totally separate and merely intermingled with the dog's primary color.

TEMPERAMENT AND BEHAVIOR

Without a doubt, the most important characteristic of any dog is a good temperament. While some breeds are known for having an inherently amiable nature, dog owners must always remember that both genetics and environment play important roles in a dog's disposition. For this reason, it is absolutely imperative that dogs bred together are both carefully selected and well matched to each other. The dogs chosen for breeding programs are considered desirable because of their impressive physical characteristics that will help produce puppies who similarly match the breed standard as closely as possible. If the resulting temperament is not also given priority in the planning, however, the breeder—and ultimately the dogs' future owners—will be left with animals who make just as inferior pets as they do show dogs.

Some of the words used most often to describe the English Cocker Spaniel temperament include "cheerful," "sweet," and "playful." After spending just a short amount of time with an English Cocker, one can quickly add "intelligent," "loyal," and "adaptable" to this list of admirable traits. English Cockers make playful pets, impressive athletes, or first-rate show dogs—and in some cases, all three. Indeed, the best description of the English Cocker Spaniel may be "well rounded." They can share their lives with a variety of people and bring the same amount of pleasure and companionship to each one of them.

Intelligence and Curiosity

English Cocker Spaniels are very intelligent animals, capable of learning a wide range of commands and further developing many

To Each His Own

The English Cocker Spaniel and the American Cocker Spaniel share many personality traits. There are, however, a few marked differences between the two breeds. For instance, many breeders insist that the English Cocker is a much calmer dog. English Cockers are also generally more dependent on human companionship than their American cousins. Owners must be careful not to allow them to become possessive, or aggression can ensue. This makes early training an important step. Additionally, American Cockers are prone to submissive and/or excitable wetting (leaking urine when in the presence of a superior dog or human or when overly excited). English Cockers, on the other hand, usually do not suffer from this problem.

Dogs Are Individuals

Breeders can frequently offer insight into the differences between individual English Cockers. Solid liver English Cockers, for example, are believed by some to be especially sensitive; my breeder calls them "tenderhearted." Black and white parti-colored dogs are thought to be spitfires. In contrast, the liver and white parti-colored pups are considered mellower, while black dogs and buff dogs have reputations for being even more laid back. Of course, these are only opinions, but bear in mind that they are the opinions of those who know the breed best.

of their natural talents and behaviors. Cultivating these innate abilities can lead to any number of enjoyable pastimes, including therapy work, obedience trials, and competitive tracking. Of course, you don't necessarily need to involve your English Cocker in structured hobbies like these to make use of his intellect; you can also take advantage of his clever mind by simply playing together in your own backyard.

English Cockers are naturally curious. They thrive on being included in nearly everything that goes on around them, and if they must, they will force themselves in on the action. Perhaps this accounts for the breed's insatiable thirst for learning. Whether you are throwing a ball around outside or teaching your dog what it means to heel, he will never cease to surprise you with his undying devotion to accomplishing his biggest goal: pleasing you.

Although most English Cockers share many universal qualities, they also tend to possess very unique individual personalities. Some are bashful, while others seem extremely outgoing almost from birth. Some seem to burst at the seams with energy, whereas others are satisfied with just a daily jaunt or two around the block. Certain English Cockers are stubborn, whereas others are more accommodating.

IS THE ENGLISH COCKER SPANIEL RIGHT FOR YOU?

Shortly before my husband and I brought our Cocker Spaniel, Molly, home from the breeder, we met with Molly and her littermates one last time. Our breeder and her husband were gracious enough to let us visit for the bulk of an entire afternoon, playing with the puppies and talking about our mutual love of dogs—Cocker Spaniels in particular. After kissing our little girl goodbye and telling her that we'd be back for her soon, the breeder's husband asked us rather nonchalantly, "Are you early risers?" Before either my husband or I could answer, he then offered with a smile, "If you aren't, you *will* be." It seemed Molly and her siblings woke reliably at five o'clock each and every morning.

During our drive home, my husband and I discussed all the important things—how beautiful Molly's markings were, how impressed we were when she voluntarily left the room to pee on her newspapers the breeder had set out in the adjoining room, and

Each English Cocker is a unique individual with his own unique personality traits and quirks.

how neither of us could wait until it was finally time to bring her home. When we pulled into our driveway nearly a half hour later, I asked hesitantly, "What do you think about this five o'clock in the morning business?" My husband responded with an equal mix of humor and sincerity. "Well, we'll just have to break her of that."

After being the proud owners of this darling little black and white Cocker for a full two weeks, we realized that we had broken her of this habit so well, in fact, that we had seen the sunrise at least 10 of these 14 days. The training was indeed successful; my husband and I had officially been broken of our nasty habit of sleeping in until seven.

In all fairness, I must acknowledge that the housetraining process probably had a lot to do with our willingness to accommodate Molly's already ingrained habit of rising with the sun. We quickly learned that when she started fussing at 5:01 a.m., we had approximately two minutes to get dressed and get her outside before the floodgates opened. After her bladder grew and strengthened, though, we did manage to convince her that sleeping until 6:30 a.m. was at least worth trying. At two years old now, she even appears to have a fair understanding of the correlation between weekends and sleeping late, or at least sleeping *later*.

Out and About With Your English Cocker

Before walking with or exercising your English Cocker in a public place, make sure that your dog is permitted there. Not all public parks welcome dogs, and some only allow dogs to exercise in designated areas. In the country, dogs should be kept on a lead when walking along foot paths or bridle tracks, and should never be allowed off the lead near livestock of any kind.

Also, regardless of where you live or where you take your pet, a responsible dog owner will always clean up any mess made by her dog.

(Courtesy of the Cocker Spaniel Club)

Fortunately for us, Molly's roosterlike tendencies were really her only issue as a new family member. Through the process of teaching her the finer points of sleep, though, we saw just how adaptive Cocker Spaniels can be. Even as a puppy, she seemed to understand that her natural clock was a bit early for us. On weekdays, we would generally use our extra morning time to get an early start to our day, but during the weekends we tended to get up to take her for her walk and then head back to bed. As much as she always wanted to play after skipping through the dew-wet grass, on Saturdays and Sundays, she would come back to bed and quietly chew her Nylabone as we climbed back under the covers for another hour or two.

Although they can have very strong personalities, Cockers are indeed very flexible dogs when it comes to fitting into their owners' lifestyles. My parents, who own their own business, have taken their Cocker Spaniel, Jennifer, with them to work for years. When they know the workday will be extra long (a common occurrence), they also bring along her dinner, and she supervises the day's work until it's time for either dinner or a nap—whichever comes first. Both my parents and many of their customers fondly refer to Jenny as the company's production manager.

The Country Cocker and the City Cocker

English Cockers do well residing in either urban or rural settings. They require a modest amount of space, so apartments usually suit them fine, but they also take great pleasure in romping around larger areas. When properly trained, most English Cockers are not usually destructive, but watch the cover on your garbage can. If I were a betting woman, I would wager that an English Cocker nose could sniff out a half-eaten saltine buried beneath days of less tempting trash.

Keep Him Leashed!

Whether you walk your dog along a busy sidewalk or on a grassy knoll, remember the importance of using a leash. While owners are usually mindful of the dangers of running free where cars are constantly buzzing past, it is equally important to remember to keep your English Cocker leashed in suburban areas, as well. Even dogs painstakingly trained to obey their owners when off-leash can be spooked into darting into oncoming traffic. A fenced yard can offer English Cockers the best of both worlds—the ability to run free, but with the safety of a secure environment. Just be sure that your dog cannot squeeze through any breaches in the structure.

English Cockers do well in urban or rural settings.

Attention

Although most do quite well in an apartment or condominium setting, English Cockers can be quite noisy when they want to be. A dog who is left alone for long hours each day while his owner works may turn to howling or other unpleasant behaviors as a way of coping with the situation. A better alternative if you work full time or spend a significant amount of time away from home is placing your English Cocker in dog daycare.

Keeping Your English Cocker Fit as a Fiddle— Exercise Needs

English Cocker Spaniels need a moderate amount of exercise, but this can usually be accomplished

How Much Exercise Should My English Cocker Have Each Day?

Puppies need only to play in the yard at first. Once their inoculations are complete, they can have a little gentle exercise and meet the outside world. Once they are about six months old and their bone structure is more or less developed, then they can go for longer walks. They should not be allowed to become exhausted but build up their exercise routine little by little.

Most adult Cocker Spaniels will be very happy having a brisk walk for about 20 to 30 minutes morning and evening. Your Cocker will also have to go out into the yard about every four hours during the day. Many dogs enjoy playing with a ball or flying disc. This is a good way of burning off energy and it is a fun activity. Cockers will walk with their owners over considerable distances if required. Many owners enjoy long country walks at weekends.

(Courtesy of the Cocker Spaniel Club)

Multi-Species Households

Pet English Cocker Spaniels get along remarkably well with other animals—from Greyhounds to guinea pigs. Many even enjoy the company of cats. If your dog has been trained for the field, however, birds and other smaller animals may not be ideal housemates.

relatively easily through daily walks and play periods. A considerable part of the reason why English Cockers are so athletic may be due to their intense love of play. Fitness, you see, is about movement, and as anyone who has ever tried to keep up with an active English Cocker Spaniel knows, these swift creatures can move with impressive speed. The key is making physical activity part of your dog's daily routine, so that this becomes a healthy habit from the very beginning.

If you enjoy walking or running, include your dog in your own fitness plan. You will have to limit the amount of running your dog does while he is still a puppy, of course, but just getting out for a nice long walk once or twice a day can effectively fulfill your dog's daily exercise needs. You can also help meet these needs by taking your dog along for social gatherings that are part of your routine—like meeting friends at the park for a game of Frisbee or going to the beach for an evening cookout. (Most English Cockers love the beach!) In addition to moving around and having fun, your dog will benefit from the socialization that is inherent in these kinds of pastimes.

One definite benefit to exercise is the effect it usually has on a dog's tendency to act out. Excessive barking or howling, destructive tendencies, and even aggression can all be lessened just by providing your English Cocker with a positive outlet for his energy. It also helps keep him at a reasonable weight, which can prevent numerous health conditions, including arthritis, diabetes, and heart disease.

If you are physically fit, you know how invigorated exercise can make *you* feel—don't deny your dog that same dynamic sensation. If you are not as in shape as you'd like to be, consider making some changes for the better for both you and your English Cocker Spaniel. You simply couldn't ask for a more eager workout partner.

Cockers and Kids

When I was pregnant with my son, Alec, I worried periodically about how my first Cocker Spaniel, Jonathan, would react once the baby arrived. Johnny had always been an incredibly sweet and loyal dog, but he had also always been just like a child to me—an *only* child. Would he resent the baby? Would the baby be safe around him? These are the questions that passed through my mind

English Cocker Spaniels typically get along very well with children.

Should I Allow My Child to Help Care for My English Cocker?

Yes! Allowing children to help care for a pet teaches responsibility and instills a feeling of competency and accomplishment. Choose tasks appropriate for the age of your child. Even young children can be involved in some aspect of caring for an animal friend—by selecting a new toy or collar, assisting with grooming, or carrying a food can at mealtime.

The best way to teach your children how to be responsible pet caregivers is to be one yourself. This should start before you even get a pet—make sure you have realistic expectations about dog ownership, and take steps to select the right animal for your family at the right time.

As soon as you bring a pet into your family, set up and enforce rules regarding proper pet care. For example, tell your children not to pull the animal's tail, ears, or other body parts, and insist that they never tease, hit, or chase him. Teach children how to properly pick up, hold, and pet the dog—these simple lessons are essential to helping kids learn responsible animal care.

Although certain pet-care activities must be handled by adults, you can still include your children by explaining what you're doing and why. For example, when you take your pet to the veterinarian to be spayed or neutered, explain to your child how the operation not only reduces pet overpopulation but can also make your pet healthier, calmer, and more affectionate.

Also, involve your children in training activities, which not only make your pet a more well-mannered family member, but also teach your child humane treatment of animals and effective communication.

(Courtesy of the HSUS)

when I woke in the middle of the night, craving milkshakes and listening to Jonathan snore.

When my son arrived, I was ever vigilant. I never left Johnny alone with the baby, but Johnny never left me alone with him either. When Alec awoke at two in the morning, I would scoop him out of his cradle and slip into the living room to quietly feed him as he drifted back off to sleep—and each and every time Jonathan was right there by my side.

My parents' Cocker Spaniel, Jennifer, was equally dutiful around my new arrival. She would sit for what seemed like hours on end, just watching him in his cradle or portable crib. When his diaper needed changing, she was the first to know and would scratch at my leg and bark insistently. Not since Disney's Lady, who saved her masters' baby from those scheming Siamese cats, had a dog been so devoted to an infant. None of us ever relied on either Johnny's or Jenny's doting nature, but seeing the two of them react to my newborn was one of the most special things I have ever witnessed in my entire life.

Some people insist that both English and American Cocker Spaniels make terrible pets for people with kids. Indeed, the stigma these breeds began to face as a result of rampant puppy milling of American Cockers still tinges both breeds' reputations today. This is most unfortunate, for when bred responsibly and treated properly, Cocker Spaniels truly adore children. A dog's breed does not make him aggressive—his environment does. Most well-bred English Cocker Spaniels are great with kids, but as with any other breed, a certain amount of training and socialization is essential.

Of course, parents should never trust *any* dog alone with their kids, no matter how friendly the dog or how certain the owner is that the dog's temperament is reliable. Additionally, however, parents should always remember that young children (and sometimes even older ones) should never be trusted alone with a dog either. Whether intentional or not, a toddler can easily inflict a serious injury to an English Cocker Spaniel. Once provoked, the animal may then act out toward the child, and the consequences could be devastating.

3

PREPARING

for Your English Cocker Spaniel

Bringing home your new English Cocker Spaniel is a joyous event. Like planning for a baby, however, getting ready for this new arrival can seem overwhelming at first. A plethora of companies in the marketplace today produce all manner of gizmos and gadgets promising to make your life as a dog owner easier. Take care before assuming that you need all these items. By focusing on the things that matter most—the staples of dog care, if you will—and making some modest preparations within your home, you will be well ready for your English Cocker's homecoming and still have plenty of time to decide which extras will be worth a little indulgence down the road.

NEW PUPPY OR SEASONED ADULT?

The first thing you will need to know before buying a single thing is whether a puppy or an adult dog is right for you. Each has its discernible advantages, so this decision is truly a matter of which better suits the individual dog owner and lifestyle. Both can be extremely rewarding options and lead you to the dog of your dreams.

Puppy Pros and Cons

Few people can resist an English Cocker Spaniel puppy. With their soft, floppy ears and playful dispositions, English Cocker puppies seem to exemplify the canine spirit. Puppies also have very little history, and when they are carefully selected, what limited history they do have should only help the pups become happy, well-adjusted dogs.

Puppies also offer their owners multiple years of companionship. While there is no guarantee how long any dog will live, the likelihood of sharing a decade or more of your life with a dog you purchase at a young age is significantly higher than with an older dog. Quantity does not prevail over quality, of course, but these additional years may be an important factor—especially for someone who has recently lost a dog and is simply not up to the task of grieving again anytime soon.

Whether to acquire a new puppy or an adult dog is a matter of personal preference—both offer their own advantages and disadvantages.

Adult Pros and Cons

If you don't wish to go through the process of housetraining and constantly having to deter a puppy from infantile behaviors (such as chewing), perhaps an older dog is better for you. Adopting an adult dog is a more practical alternative for many older people, since puppies also demand a good amount of exhaustive play. Adult English Cockers (dogs over the age of two) are much more interested in chewing on their own toys or taking a nap rather than grabbing your shoe and challenging you to a game of chase around the dining room table for its relinquishment.

Smaller breeds tend to have longer lifespans than larger ones. You can expect an English Cocker Spaniel to live between 10 and 15 years. This makes the English Cocker a very practical choice for adoption and rescue. Some dogs are surrendered when they are barely out of the puppy stage and require only a small amount of training to become ideal pets. Others may have more involved needs, but most are still extremely viable candidates for the right homes.

If you have small children, adopting a dog with an existing tendency toward any type of aggression is not wise. In this case a brand-new puppy would be a better decision, but problems with other behavioral issues (such as housetraining or chewing) can easily be overcome in a household with older kids. Having more people around to help out with the dog's training is actually an advantage; the most important thing every dog needs is love, and the more people in the household to offer it, the better.

FINDING THE ENGLISH COCKER SPANIEL OF YOUR DREAMS

Adoption—An Overlooked Option

If you think adopting an English Cocker Spaniel may be for you, begin by calling local animal shelters. If there are no English

Yin or Yang?

Which makes a better pet—a male or female? It depends on the preferences of each individual owner. While I can honestly say that I enjoy both genders equally, this doesn't mean that there aren't differences between the two.

My breeder tells me that everyone always seems to want a female pup, and this makes sense. Male dogs in general are often vilified as being more destructive, harder to housetrain, and more aggressive. My experience? Females can be just as aggressive as their male counterparts, especially with other females; and you never know how difficult it will be to housetrain any dog. And although I myself have found males to be more destructive than females, my breeder tells me that a certain female she knows (the dam of my mother's newest American Cocker, actually) was, as a puppy, the worst chewer she has ever seen—simply incorrigible until she was at least two years old.

I have found females to be bossier, more cunning, and certainly more independent. Males, on the other hand, in my opinion are cuddlier, more clownish, and (dare I say) more "girly."

Cockers presently available, you can always leave your name and contact information so that they can alert you of one's arrival. Also, keep an eye on the newspaper classifieds. You never know where you might find an English Cocker Spaniel in need of someone just like you.

If you don't have any luck with this route, it may be time to contact the English Cocker Spaniel Club of America Rescue. A volunteer should be able to direct you to an English Cocker rescue group near you, and ultimately a dog in need of a new home. Several such groups serve various regions of the country.

Breed-specific rescue organizations can be expedient resources for people looking to adopt purebred dogs. Like your local animal shelter, a rescue organization works to help animals in need of a second chance by finding them loving homes. Unlike the protocol of shelters, though, the dogs are kept in foster care until the right owner for each one comes along. What most sets a rescue group apart, however, is its concentration on a single breed. This streamlined focus offers prospective owners a wide range of knowledge and support from people who have been involved with the breed for years.

Selecting an Adoptive Dog

When selecting an adoptive dog, approach the situation at least somewhat as if you were buying a puppy. Although countless animals out there are in need, you should strive to choose the one that best suits your individual circumstances so that you may best fulfill the dog's specific needs. You may wish you could take them all home, but good intentions and sympathy can only go so far. You need to be able to honor your commitment to the animal you select and ensure that he will never be left homeless again.

This doesn't mean that you have to be an expert on dog ownership. You usually won't need extensive knowledge of obedience training—or even a history with English Cocker Spaniels in particular (although any amount of experience will definitely be helpful). A basic understanding of dog care and a willingness to learn what you don't already know is usually enough, provided that you have the proper time to devote to the task. Dogs with more complicated needs, though, will require owners with comparable knowledge.

Through fostering these dogs, the rescue groups are able to evaluate each dog's needs, identify any existing problems, and (if necessary) establish a plan to start correcting these issues immediately. Sometimes new owners will need to pick up where the foster owners leave off, but not always. Many rescued dogs in need of remedial housetraining, for example, are already trained by the time they become ready for placement.

When you acquire an English Cocker, make sure you are willing and able to care for your new pet for the rest of his life.

A common age for English Cockers in rescue is two years old—the age that one rescue friend of mine calls the "rebellious teenager" period. Behavioral issues in an English Cocker at this age are often easily corrected with obedience training—again, sometimes even before the dog becomes available for adoption. English Cockers between the ages of five and seven also enter rescue frequently and are surrendered for a myriad of reasons. Sometimes there is nothing at all wrong with the dog, and usually any problems that do exist are either correctable or manageable. Additionally, rescues take in a fair number of senior English Cockers; these are often ideal pets for people who work, because these older dogs have moved beyond the chewing stage and are also far less boisterous than puppies or young adults.

Many wonderful English Cocker Spaniels are in need of committed owners. Some have been given up for reasons completely unrelated to their behavior, such as divorces, financial hardships, or moves to housing where no-dog policies are in place. Others may suffer from health problems (either minor or severe) or present serious behavioral challenges. Talk to the people from the rescue group, and ask as many questions as possible. Together you can decide whether you might be able to change an English Cocker Spaniel's life (and your own) by providing him with something he has never had—a permanent home.

The Screening Process

Rescue groups take their work very seriously, and as a result, they usually have an understandably extensive screening process. In addition to filling out a detailed application form, you may likely be required to agree to a home visit from a rescue representative before you can be approved. All people who live in your household (especially children) need to be present for this visit. You will also be asked to provide references relating to your history as a pet owner (veterinarians top the list of desirable references).

Some groups require that you sign either a temporary or permanent restraint agreement, stating that you will always keep your English Cocker on a leash or within a fenced yard whenever he is outside. Nearly all groups have a contract demanding that you return the dog to the rescue group if for any reason you cannot continue to care for him in the future. Most groups will ask that

Make sure you acquire your English Cocker from a reputable breeder.

you keep in touch with the organization, making contact at least once within the next year and letting someone know if your address or phone number changes. This way, the group and all its resources will be available to you for as long as you own the dog.

Try not to be intimidated by any of these steps, as each is vital in helping you find the best dog for you and your current lifestyle. While the screening process is first and foremost a means of weeding out unsuitable owners, it is also an effective way to make the best match possible between a dog and his potential owner—a rescue group's most important goal. Rest assured that if you are the right person for an English Cocker Spaniel, you are the right person for one of these dogs.

Breeders

If your heart is set on buying a puppy, you need to find a suitable source, such as a reputable English Cocker Spaniel breeder. Depending on where you live, locating an English Cocker breeder can be a difficult task, but finding a trustworthy one can be even more challenging. Of course, many responsible people throughout the US strive to produce quality English Cocker pups. Unfortunately, there are also many unscrupulous individuals whose sole concern is making money—even at the expense of their own dogs' health and safety.

Puppy Mills

Puppy mills are large companies that breed mass quantities of purebred dogs. Dogs at these facilities are usually housed in small, overcrowded cages often piled several rows high. Because producing numerous puppies is the main objective, dogs are bred at every opportunity, beginning when the dogs have barely reached sexual maturity. In many cases, dogs are born within just a year of their parents.

Temperament, one of the biggest concerns of reputable breeders, is also compromised in puppy mills. Lacking adequate human socialization, dogs often end up with an array of behavioral or emotional issues. Although these dogs usually come complete with American Kennel Club (AKC) paperwork, you will rarely be able to meet a dog's parents to get a feel for what the animal's temperament will likely be.

Since puppy mills have come under increased scrutiny in recent years, they have been forced to be more creative with their marketing techniques. Frequently, the English Cocker Spaniel puppies you see advertised for sale online or in your local newspaper are actually puppy mill dogs. The smoke and mirrors can be quite impressive, giving the appearance of a legitimate and caring operation. A telltale sign, though, is a common phone number for several different breeds. The only true way to make sure you are buying from a responsible breeder is to visit the kennel personally.

Good to Know

Health, temperament, and conformation qualities should be a breeder's top priorities.

"Backyard" Breeders

Good breeders do exist, but they too must be painstakingly selected from all the others. The letters "AKC" do not necessarily indicate a responsible breeder. Anyone who wants to mate two purebred English Cocker Spaniels registered with the AKC can technically become an English Cocker breeder.

Sadly, owners who think their pets have what it takes to produce quality English Cocker pups usually lack the judgment and experience to make this kind of decision. In most cases, the resulting litters consist of dogs with less than desirable physical traits—or worse, dogs with an increased risk of multiple health problems. While some may be well intentioned, these owners— often called "backyard breeders"are making some very ignorant and dangerous mistakes. Those who continue to breed with no regard for the outcome (even after furnished with all the facts) deserve the same disdain as puppy mills.

Hobby Breeders

Hobby breeders are experienced dog owners who breed dogs, but not as a primary source of income—their greatest goal is the betterment of their chosen breed. Occasionally, a hobby breeder may specialize in two different breeds, but any more than that is very rare. Health, temperament, and conformation qualities are a

Worth the Wait

If all goes well with your chosen breeder, you may still need to wait a while for an available puppy. Perhaps the breeder has other people before you on the waiting list, or maybe another litter won't be arriving for a few months. Responsible breeders will not breed their dogs at every opportunity. Most hobby breeders usually raise only one or two litters each year. If you are impressed with what you have seen, try to be patient, as your English Cocker Spaniel puppy should be well worth the wait.

Keep in mind that just because the breeder has a long waiting list, this does not mean that all these people will actually purchase pups. If someone is holding out for a specific color or gender, or if for any reason that person's circumstances have changed, that cute little English Cocker puppy you've had your eye on just might become available.

hobby breeder's top priorities. This does not mean that you won't pay a fair price for one of their dogs, but it is unlikely that this ethical breeder will break even after raising an entire litter.

Finding an English Cocker Spaniel Breeder

Hobby breeders are generally considered the cream of the breeding crop, but they can be difficult to find using mainstream methods such as the phone book or other advertisements. Many actually prefer to be a bit more elusive, as this can help discourage impulsive people and other less than desirable owners from buying their dogs. Instead of actively soliciting business, hobby breeders will usually keep waiting lists of people looking for English Cocker pups and then contact them when a litter is on the way.

The best way to locate a trustworthy English Cocker Spaniel breeder is by contacting the AKC or the English Cocker Spaniel Club and asking for a referral in your area. Of course, membership in the AKC, breed clubs, or any other organization is not by itself enough reason to select a specific breeder, but it is an excellent start. Many English Cocker breeders are actively involved with conformation showing, obedience trials, agility, or a combination of these activities. Some breeders are even current or retired AKC judges. Although participation in these kinds of events isn't imperative, being a part of the English Cocker Spaniel advanced training community is often a good sign that a breeder is knowledgeable and experienced.

Another productive means of discovering the best breeders in your area is attending a local dog show. When the English Cocker owners and handlers aren't busy (usually after their dogs are done competing in the ring), introduce yourself and ask them to tell you whom they would recommend as a good breeder. English Cocker Spaniel enthusiasts tend to be a friendly bunch of people who are drawn to those who share their interest in the breed. They are also a wonderful source for information about the breed, so use this time to ask any other questions you may have, and be sure to listen carefully to their answers.

After You Find a Breeder

Once you locate a potential breeder, you should make contact and arrange to meet at the breeder's home at a mutually convenient time. You will also want to meet some of her dogs before deciding to purchase a puppy. If the breeder presently has a pregnant female or pups under the age of four weeks, you may be asked to wait a short time before visiting. Do not be offended by this, but rather be reassured by the fact that the breeder is putting her dogs' health first.

A good breeder will be just as insistent about meeting you before agreeing to sell you a dog. You will be asked many questions in the beginning, relating to your experience with dogs and your current lifestyle. Typical questions are:

- What breeds have you previously owned?
- What other animals do you own now?
- How much time will you have to devote to a new puppy?
- Have you ever surrendered a dog to a shelter or rescue group?
- Do you rent? (If you rent your home, you may be required to show proof that your landlord will allow you to own a dog.)

You should have a lot of questions for the breeder you plan to acquire your pet from—and she should have a lot of questions for you.

While this may seem like an interrogation of sorts, keep in mind that these are all legitimate concerns for a breeder who wants the best for her pups.

You will want to ask many questions, also. Don't be afraid to ask for references from other people who have purchased puppies from the breeder, and make the effort to contact them. Ask these owners if the breeder provided them with ample follow-up after the sale, if they have had any problems with their dogs, and whether they would use the same breeder again. Just like other English Cocker enthusiasts, most of these people will be more than happy to share their experiences with you—both good and bad.

The First Visit

Once the breeder feels the pups are ready to meet you, start planning your first visit, but take precautions not to bring any illnesses into the breeder's home. Refrain from visiting any places where a great number of dogs are gathered before you meet the new litter. For example, without even realizing it, you could carry the parvovirus in on your shoes after attending a dog show or walking through a park. Parvo is extremely hardy and can exist in ground contaminated with fecal matter for several months, but it only takes about 10 days for an infected dog to show symptoms of this deadly disease. Since dogs cannot be vaccinated against parvo until they are at least six weeks old, young puppies are extremely vulnerable.

When you visit a breeder's home, first and foremost look for signs that the dogs are much-loved pets. Even if the breeder specializes in show dogs, these dogs too should be considered a part of the family. Are there toys around? Are the dogs kept inside the home or in a separate area? What kind of rapport does the breeder have with her animals?

Trust your instincts, especially those that raise any red flags. A rightful cause for concern is a breeder who seems more interested in the money than the other details of your meeting, but anything that sets you on edge should be considered. Even if everything else about a breeder seems acceptable, if you simply don't like the person, this alone could be enough of a reason to keep looking. If you need advice down the road, your breeder should be the first person you contact, so it's reasonable to want someone who is friendly and approachable.

Paperwork

Before you take your new puppy home, your breeder should have you read and sign a written agreement that clearly outlines the responsibilities of both parties. The breeder's responsibilities will likely include taking the dog back if for any reason you are unable to care for him in the future. You might be allowed to find the dog a new home with the breeder's approval, however.

Unless you are purchasing a show dog, you will probably be required to spay or neuter your English Cocker Spaniel. If you are buying a show dog, you may be required to spay or neuter the animal once he finishes his conformation career.

The breeder should provide you with a written pedigree for your English Cocker puppy, including the litter's dam, sire, and ancestors. The dog's bloodlines and inheritable traits should be explained at this time, if not sooner.

Be Aware of Health Issues

Beware of a breeder who is unwilling to acknowledge or discuss common English Cocker afflictions, as every dog breed is prone to one kind of health issue or another. The fact that many spaniels suffer from cataracts is not enough reason for most people to reconsider buying one, but you must be certain that the breeder's dogs have been tested for these genetic problems, and that any dogs who test positive are eliminated from the breeding program.

The breeder should also offer some kind of guarantee (up to a certain age) against the most common genetic health issues of the breed—namely eye and skeletal problems. Keep in mind that even the best breeders can produce dogs with problems; the most they can do is offer the option of replacement. In this situation, however, many breeders will allow you to keep both the replacement dog and your original English Cocker if that is what you want. If the problem is of such magnitude that you feel you must give up your dog, however, the breeder should then be willing to take the animal back and provide you with a new dog once one becomes available.

Finally, you should be provided with your puppy's immunization record to date. Bring this with you to your dog's first veterinary appointment. Your breeder may give you a list of recommended veterinarians in your area, but you should not be required to use a specific doctor. Some breeders also send each puppy home with a care package, including a suggested feeding schedule, literature about dog care and training, and in some cases, even a small amount of food and a toy or two.

A breeder may wait to provide you with the AKC registration paperwork until your dog has been spayed or neutered. Again, don't be offended by this, as making certain that you have fulfilled this part of your contract is another sign that you have chosen

A breeder may withhold your new Cocker's AKC registration papers until you have your new pet spayed or neutered.

Registering Your English Cocker Spaniel

American Kennel Club: Registering your new English Cocker Spaniel puppy with the AKC is an easy and fun task. Your breeder should provide you with the necessary form, which will include both the dam and sire's registration numbers, as well as with your puppy's number. All you need to do is fill in your name and address, along with the name you have chosen for your dog.

Most breeders require that their kennel name precede the puppy's name. For example, if the kennel's name is Happy Tails, and you want to name your dog Joy, the full registered name would be written "Happy Tails' Joy". The full name cannot exceed 30 letters. (Spaces between words, apostrophes, and hyphens are counted in this total.) You may choose a longer name for your dog's AKC paperwork, such as "Pride and Joy", but use just Joy or PJ for his nickname.

There is a non-refundable application fee for registration. You can mail this payment along with your completed paperwork to the AKC or register online at www.akc.org. There, you will find detailed instructions, including a first-time user's guide and checklist for the organization's online registration service.

Kennel Club (KC): In England, the complete registration of a litter with the KC is the responsibility of the breeder. During this process, the breeder will also officially name all the puppies. Each buyer is provided with a registration certificate for the puppy, complete with a section for the transfer of ownership that should be returned to the KC after the sale. A buyer should make sure that the breeder has signed this section of the document before forwarding it to the KC.

a responsible breeder. Since most English Cockers are ready to be altered by five to six months of age, you will be receiving the paperwork before you know it.

PREPARING YOUR HOME FOR THE NEW ARRIVAL

Puppy-proofing your house is actually a lot like preparing a home for a baby. Just like small children, English Cocker Spaniel puppies are incredibly curious individuals, and nearly every item that attracts their fleeting attention goes right into their mouths. Tiny objects that may be swallowed pose particular concern, but more substantial items can be dangerous for your dog as well.

Keeping things neat and in their place is a great first step— especially if you care about your shoes! Anything left out in the open is at the mercy of your teething puppy's impulse to chew. This doesn't mean that you must keep all your belongings put away all the time; it just means that your dog cannot be allowed access to them. I highly recommended investing in a baby gate (or even two or three) for those areas of your home that will either permanently or temporarily be off limits to your dog. In the beginning, it is wise to place gates near any stairways, but you may also find them useful for blocking off access to carpeted rooms and children's bedrooms. A five-year-old child cannot be counted on to pick up every tiny game or puzzle piece, but you can certainly depend on your English Cocker Spaniel puppy to find it if given the opportunity.

Once you have determined the areas needing puppy-proofing, remove all dangerous items that your puppy can reach. These may include low-lying electrical cords, plants, and even the garbage can. More than one curious English Cocker pup has ended up in the veterinary hospital after indulging in "dumpster diving." Also, be sure that all doors and windows are securely closed.

If your windows are covered with Venetian blinds, take extra care in tying the cords safely out of reach—or even better, consider removing them entirely. Even the inner cords running through the slats of these types of blinds can strangle a small child or animal.

Dangers lurk everywhere and often in places you might never suspect. Constantly be on the lookout for anything that might pose a threat to your dog's safety. By doing so, you just might save his life.

SUPPLIES

Crate

To crate or not to crate? This is a common question among dog owners, and there is no universally correct answer. A crate may serve as an effective housetraining tool, a safe location for your English Cocker Spaniel puppy when you are not at home, or a quiet refuge for your dog during nap time. It may even fulfill all three purposes. Whether or not you ever plan on closing its door, though, I strongly recommend investing in this item.

I am no stranger to the opinion that crating is cruel. At one time I believed this myself—until, that is, my own American Cocker Spaniel puppy, Molly, began seeking out a place of her own. Unfortunately, her preferred spot was under my desk among the computer peripherals' various cords and other potentially dangerous gear. No matter what I did, I could not convince her that

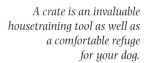

A crate is an invaluable housetraining tool as well as a comfortable refuge for your dog.

this was not the place for her. After resisting the idea for several days, I finally decided to give the crate a try, and this may well be one of the best decisions I have ever made for my dogs.

From the day I placed the crate in our home—in the same room as my desk, since that was obviously where Molly wanted to be—the crate has replaced the cave-like solace that my desk provided, but with safer, more comfortable surroundings.

Molly's crate is one of her most treasured possessions—right alongside the pink stuffed mouse I brought her when she was just weeks old and still at the breeder's. She enters her crate all on her own whenever she feels like taking a break from the household commotion, if she has a special treat she wishes to savor privately, or if she hears the rattle of her metal crate door. Her crate is obviously something she values a great deal.

Why Crates Are Useful

A crate can speed up the housetraining process significantly. Since dogs are by nature very clean animals, they prefer not to soil the area they occupy. By keeping a puppy in his crate when you

10 Tips for a Safe Household

1. Be aware of the plants you have in your house and in your pet's yard. The ingestion of azalea, oleander, mistletoe, sago palm, Easter lily, or yew plant material by an animal could be fatal.

2. When cleaning your house, never allow your pet access to the area where cleaning agents are used or stored. Cleaning agents have a variety of properties. Some may only cause a mild stomach upset, while others could cause severe burns of the tongue, mouth, and stomach.

3. When using rat or mouse baits, ant or roach traps, or snail and slug baits, place the products in areas that are inaccessible to your animals. Most baits contain sweet-smelling inert ingredients, such as jelly, peanut butter, and sugars, which can be very attractive to your pet.

4. Never give your animal any medications unless under the direction of your veterinarian. Many medications that are used safely by humans can be deadly when administered inappropriately to a dog.

5. Keep all prescription and over-the-counter drugs out of your pets' reach, preferably in closed cabinets. Pain killers, cold medicines, anti-cancer drugs, antidepressants, vitamins, and diet pills are common examples of human medication that could be potentially lethal even in small dosages. One regular strength ibuprofen (200 mg) could cause stomach ulcers in a 10-pound (4.5 kg) dog.

6. Never leave chocolates unattended. Approximately one-half ounce or less of baking chocolate per pound (.45 kg) of body weight can cause problems. Even small amounts can cause pancreatic ailments.

7. Many common household items have been shown to be lethal in certain species. Miscellaneous items that are highly toxic even in low quantities include pennies, mothballs, potpourri oils, fabric softener sheets, automatic dish detergents, batteries, homemade play dough (due to high quantity of salt), winter heat source agents like hand or foot warmers, cigarettes, coffee grounds, and alcoholic drinks.

8. All automotive products such as oil, gasoline, and antifreeze (ethylene glycol) should be stored in areas away from pet access. As little as one teaspoon of antifreeze can be deadly to a 20-pound (9 kg) dog.

9. Before buying or using flea products on your pet or in your household, contact your veterinarian to discuss what types of flea products are recommended for your pet. Read all information before using a product on your animals or in your home, and always follow label instructions. Also, when using a fogger or a house spray, make sure to remove all pets from the area for the time period specified on the container. If you are uncertain about the usage of any product, contact the manufacturer or your veterinarian to clarify the directions before using the product.

10. When treating your lawn or garden with fertilizers, herbicides, or insecticides, always keep your animals away from the area until the area dries completely. Discuss usage of products with the manufacturer. Always store such products in an area that will ensure no possible pet exposure.

(Courtesy of the AAHA and Healthypet.com)

What the Crate Isn't

Although the crate can be an incredibly useful item for both dogs and owners, it is not a place to keep your English Cocker Spaniel for long periods of time. If your dog will be spending most days at home alone, he should not be left in his crate for more than a few hours at a time. Ideally, he should be afforded a chance to relieve himself and get some exercise around midday. If you cannot make it home at this time, consider hiring a dog walker or asking a neighbor to stop by for this purpose. Your English Cocker will also need a potty break both before you leave the house and when you return. Getting in a short but lively exercise session before your departure each day will also help him acclimate to your routine, since he will look forward to resting a bit after such a workout.

cannot keep a close eye on him, you will decrease the likelihood of housetraining accidents and empower your English Cocker with early success.

If you plan to board your English Cocker during vacations or other times you need to be away from home overnight, having a crate at home can help prepare him for the kennel experience. Although many boarding facilities offer walk-in sized kennels, the logistics are very similar. A dog who has never been inside a crate will find it difficult to acclimate to this new concept while under the added stress of being away from his owner.

Crate Selection

When selecting a crate, keep your English Cocker's future lifestyle in mind. Will your dog accompany you when you take vacations or travel to visit relatives? Where will you be placing the crate? Also, consider what, if anything, you already know about your dog's personality. Is your puppy a voracious chewer? Does he tend to seek out darker places to be alone or prefer to be involved in nearly every family activity? The answers to all these questions should affect your choice.

In addition to being extremely portable, a collapsible wire crate offers a more sociable animal a 360-degree view of its surroundings. On the other hand, if your dog's crate will be placed in a high-traffic area of your home, this might offer interaction and excitement, even for the most outgoing dog.

Plastic crates are a more economical alternative, but they don't offer the same versatility as wire. You can always toss a towel or blanket over a wire crate for privacy, for example, and remove it when no longer needed, but plastic crates offer no such option.

Plastic is also more vulnerable to the destructive gnawing of teething puppies.

Speaking of chewing, when shopping for a crate, you may notice that a number of very attractive crates are available made from all kinds of enticing materials—everything from fabric to wicker. While no one can deny the visual appeal of many of these cozy-looking lairs, the word "crate" seems a bit of a stretch. These eccentric variations may work wonderfully for style-savvy owners with perfectly behaved adult dogs, but they are not at all practical for a puppy or any dog with a tendency to gnaw on his surroundings. If you just can't resist indulging in one of these fashion-friendly havens for your English Cocker Spaniel, consider investing in a conventional crate first, and save this more ornate item for when he is fully grown and more reliable.

No matter which type of crate you select, you will need to purchase a padded liner for your English Cocker's warmth and comfort. A wide selection of liners in various styles and materials is available at most pet supply stores, including orthopedic versions for older or arthritic dogs. Of course, a folded blanket will accommodate your dog equally well, but bear in mind that you will spend a fair amount of time folding and refolding it.

Don't Force It

Some dogs tend not to do well with crates, no matter how much time or patience an owner may offer. Puppies who spent most of their early weeks inside crates may have a profound fear of being kept in any such enclosure. These puppies are also unlikely to benefit from the housetraining advantages of the crate because necessity has caused them to overcome their instinctive distaste for defecating where they also eat and sleep.

Crates and Travel

If you plan to fly with your English Cocker, you will need a plastic crate because airlines do not allow animals to be transported in the collapsible varieties. Airlines do provide their own sturdy carriers for traveling pets, but these can be rather expensive and will, of course, be completely foreign to your English Cocker. Air travel can be nerve-racking enough for an animal without the additional stress of a strange environment. Although more airlines are now permitting a small number of dogs to fly within the plane's cabin on each flight, most English Cocker Spaniels unfortunately don't fall under the weight limit for this new allowance.

If your travel is limited to driving distances, either type of crate should suit your needs. To help ensure your English Cocker's safety (and to prevent automobile accidents), never allow him to roam freely inside your vehicle while riding—especially not in the front seat, since airbags can be just as deadly to pets as they are to small children. A canine safety harness may be used with your vehicle's seatbelt, but a crate is always a safer option. The crate also

Your English Cocker will appreciate comfortable, padded material to relax on in—or out of—his crate.

provides your dog with a comfortable home-away-from-home for any trip.Most crates are sold with a small set of dishes that can be mounted on the inside of the door. If the style you chose does not include these attachable items, it is wise to pick them up separately. Not only will you need to provide your pet with access to water whenever traveling by plane, but you might also find that feeding him inside his crate is convenient—especially if other animals live within your home. For the dog who is still even a little bit leery of the crate, establishing a connection between food and the crate can have a positive effect on his adjustment.

Another item that will be a near necessity if you do plan to travel with your English Cocker Spaniel is a crate dolly. Imagine catching a flight while carrying several pieces of luggage and your English Cocker's massive crate. Just the crate alone would be too cumbersome for most people. A crate dolly will help you cruise through the airport in no time flat. Many owners who show their English Cockers or attend other regular canine events with them also find this item extremely helpful.

Food & Water Dishes

As most owners know, providing your dog with a high-quality diet is one of the most basic factors for his health and longevity, but the dishes in which you place your English Cocker's food can also impact his health.

Traveling With Your English Cocker Spaniel

Traveling long distances can be hard on your dog, but there are some things you can do to help make such trips more enjoyable and safer for your best friend. Here are some suggestions from the Humane Society of the United States (HSUS).

- When packing, don't forget your pet's food, food and water dishes, bedding, leash, collar and tags, grooming supplies, and a first-aid kit and any medications. Also, always have a container of drinking water with you.

- Your pet should wear a sturdy collar with ID tags throughout the trip. The tags should have both your permanent address and telephone number and an address and telephone number where you or a contact can be reached during your travels.

- Traveling can be upsetting to your pet's stomach. Take along ice cubes, which are easier on your pet than large amounts of water. Keep feeding to a minimum during travel. (Provide a light meal two to three hours before you leave if you are traveling by car, or four to six hours before departure if traveling by air.) Allow small amounts of water periodically in the hours before the trip.

- Carry a current photograph of your pet with you. If he is lost during a trip, a photograph will make it easier for others (airline employees, the police, shelter workers, and others) to help you find him.

Three basic types of dog dishes are available in most pet supply stores: plastic, ceramic, and stainless steel. Each has its own advantages, but some choices are generally better than others.

Plastic

Plastic dishes, while highly durable, can cause a condition in dogs called contact dermatitis. Although the term sounds a bit contrived, this is a very real contact dermatitis caused by an antioxidant found in plastic or rubber bowls. When a dog eats or drinks from a plastic dish, this antioxidant causes the dog's nose and lips to lose their pigment over time. It can also cause the skin in these areas to become inflamed and irritated. Contact your veterinarian if your dog's nose or lips seem swollen or sore. The irritation can be resolved, but the discoloration may be permanent.

Ceramic

Ceramic dishes come in a variety of attractive colors and

When traveling with your English Cocker, he should wear a sturdy collar with ID tags and should be on leash wherever you go.

designs—you can probably even find a set that perfectly matches your kitchen. Ceramic is considerably more delicate than other available materials, however. If your enthusiastic English Cocker is the type to remind you when it's dinnertime by giving his dish a shove, ceramic might not be your best option. Also, since your dog's dishes need to be washed daily, they will also be handled a great deal. You'd be amazed at how many little pieces just one ceramic bowl can shatter into when it hits a tile floor.

Another concern with ceramic dishes is lead content—improperly glazed ceramic dog bowls can contain lead. Although the standards for human use have been raised to eliminate this threat to people, ceramic pet dishes do not have to meet the same criteria. If you buy ceramic dishes for your English Cocker, be sure they are labeled "high fire" and "table quality" for this reason.

Stainless Steel

Of the three choices, stainless steel offers the best combination of durability, safety, and ease of use. Stainless steel dishes are available in multiple different styles and sizes, many with rubber bottoms that help keep the dishes firmly in place during use. These rubber rings are usually removable for easy cleaning. I recommend purchasing two sets so that your dog always has a clean set when the other is being washed.

Outdoor Water Dish

If you provide your dog with an outdoor water dish, consider using a heated or temperature-regulated bowl that keeps the water cool but prevents it from freezing. Never allow your dog to drink from a metal dish outside when the temperature is extremely low, as your dog's tongue could easily become stuck to the interior.

Leash & Collar

Before you bring your puppy home for the first time, ask your breeder to measure his neck so that you can arrive prepared with a collar that fits properly. If you need to purchase a puppy collar, and you can't seem to find one small enough, check the cat aisle of your local pet supply store.

Your breeder may tell you that she will provide your pup with his first collar. If this is the case, don't bother purchasing a second in this size, as your dog might easily outgrow it before he even gets the chance to wear it. (Within just a few months, you will be amazed when you look at the teeny collar your English Cocker Spaniel puppy wore for his milestone ride home.)

Choosing a Collar

The best strategy when selecting a collar for your dog is to bring him with you to the store to try on a number of different styles and sizes. Like all other canine accessories, collars and leashes come in a huge variety of colors, fabrics, and designs. This is all secondary, however, to a good fit. When your English Cocker is wearing his collar, you should be able to slip two fingers between his neck and the collar. Anything too loose or too tight can be dangerous, so don't be afraid to seek the help of a sales associate. They help owners with this issue all the time.

Once you determine your dog's size, the next matter of business will be the material. Leather wears best, but it is usually the most expensive choice, so you may want to postpone investing in this until your dog has reached his full size—around the age of 8 to 10 months. Cotton and nylon are both more affordable alternatives, wear considerably well, and are also washable.

Another smart option is a collar containing reflective material, which will enable others to see your dog no matter what time of day you are out with him. However, although collars of this kind are easy to find and quite affordable, a roll of reflective tape will serve the purpose just as well, and you can even add some of it to your own clothing or accessories for added safety.

Harness

Some English Cocker owners prefer to use a harness instead of a collar. This is truly a matter of personal preference. If your dog tends to pull on the leash when you walk together, a harness can help prevent him from injuring his neck or throat while you work on this issue.

Most harnesses are based on a dog's chest measurement. To determine your dog's size, place the tape around his chest, just behind his front legs. As with the collar, you should be able to comfortably fit two fingers between your dog and the apparatus. Although both collars and harnesses are usually adjustable, there is often more range involved with the latter.

Plastic food dishes are very durable but can cause contact dermatitis in your dog over time. In general, food and water dishes made of stainless steel are ideal for your pet.

What Not to Wear

I strongly advise against choke collars. These collars that loop and tighten around your dog's neck may be constructed of either

metal or nylon and are commonly referred to as "choke chains." The more the dog pulls, the more the choke hold tightens—putting him at considerable risk of injury. If you are among those trying to teach proper leash walking behavior, talk to your veterinarian or dog trainer about better ways to accomplish this task.

Although collars that tighten are the most dangerous, even conventional collars can pose a potential strangulation hazard under certain circumstances. If your English Cocker will be wearing his collar at all times, be sure that the one you select has breakaway technology, which causes the collar to break apart when it undergoes sufficient tension. It just might save your dog's life someday.

Leashes

Like collars and harnesses, leashes are available in a stunning array of materials and designs. You will want something strong enough for a dog between 28 and

32 pounds (13 and 14.5 kg)—your English Cocker's ideal weight at adulthood—and long enough to provide adequate walking space. A sufficient length is usually between 6 and 8 feet (1.8 and 2.4 m), even with a taller owner. Leashes made of chain tend to be too heavy for this relatively small breed, but leather, nylon, and cotton are all suitable choices.

An extendable leash provides an enormous amount of flexibility for both an English Cocker Spaniel and his owner. Available in lengths of up to 26 feet (7.9 m), these plastic-covered reels can retract to just a meter or less long whenever necessary. This is ideal if you walk your dog in an urban area during the week, but enjoy going to the park or out hiking on the weekend. These versatile leashes can also come in handy while training your English Cocker to come when called. They are available in a variety of colors, lengths, and styles—many with lightweight, ergonomic handles. Investing in this one item will save you both money and space, as it is quite literally several leashes in one.

The Cocker Water Bowl

In your search for the perfect set of dishes, you may encounter something called a "Cocker water bowl." This stainless steel bowl is essentially the same as any other stainless bowl on the market, except that it is noticeably narrower at the top. The purpose of this difference is to keep your dog's ears out of his water. Many owners find this unique design helpful, but how well the bowl works for you will depend on the height and width of the bowl at the top in relation to the length of your dog's ears.

Clothing

Another item you may wish to consider if you live in a colder climate is a sweater or coat for your dog. English Cocker Spaniels love being outdoors regardless of the season; mine especially enjoy playing in the snow. I have to virtually drag them back inside even in New England's most frigid temperatures. Some may argue that English Cockers don't need cold weather clothing due to their built-in coats, but seeing my dogs shiver (and still insist on staying outdoors) was enough to lead me to invest in two different canine winter accessories—coats and boots.

To determine your dog's coat size, measure him from collar to tail. For a long time, I preferred sweaters to coats, as the cutesy designs of most coats I'd seen appeared to be high on fashion but lacking in warmth. I find fleece coats, however, to provide more warmth than many sweaters. They also aren't as susceptible to snags from claws and teeth.

Protecting the Paws

One of the contradictions I have observed in many English Cocker Spaniels is their affection for water—on their own terms, that is. My dog Molly will actually pout if I draw a bath for anyone in the house other than her. She needs absolutely no coaxing when it is her turn to get in the tub. (My first Cocker had to be bribed with luncheon meat, mind you.) Molly also really enjoys swimming in the summer. On a rainy day, however, just the thought of getting her feathered feet wet is enough to make her pull to go back inside as soon as we set out for her walk. If your English Cocker is anything like Molly, you may consider purchasing a set of doggy boots. Some dogs will not tolerate having their feet confined within boots, but I have seen others wear them with ease. Try them on in the store to ensure both size and comfort.

A problem many owners overlook is their dogs' continual exposure to the harshest outdoor surfaces. In cold weather, this may be snow and ice—or worse, salt. In the summer, it may be hot pavement or prickly rocks and gravel. Applying paw wax can help protect your dog's paws and pads from these virtually unavoidable elements. In addition to providing your dog with a protective layer to ward off abrasions, burning, drying, and cracking, this unique product also gives him better traction when walking on ice. Although paw wax will not keep his feet dry, it will act as an invisible boot by getting between your English Cocker's vulnerable pads and any surfaces they touch. You can find paw wax at most pet supply stores.

Leather, nylon, and cotton leashes are all suitable for your English Cocker.

Toys, Toys, Toys!

All dogs need toys, but English Cocker Spaniels delight in them—especially Cocker puppies.

In addition to providing your dog with a constructive outlet for chewing (an essential activity for a healthy jaw and good tooth development), toys also offer an opportunity for both recreation and exercise. Like games and gadgets for humans, they can also be highly valued possessions that help alleviate your dog's boredom, frustration, and stress.

Of course, simply handing your dog a ball and expecting him to play alone will not do. Certain items—a Nylabone, for example—may be designed for quiet enjoyment. A Frisbee, on the other hand, demands at least two active players for the game. From your English Cocker Spaniel's perspective, the best thing about a squeak toy is that exhilarating feeling of taunting his master with it and then running away before she can take it.

When you give your dog a toy, you are also teaching him which items within your household are and are not acceptable for his teething pleasure. To help him learn the rules, only allow him to play with his own toys. If you come home from work to discover that your cross-trainers have been munched down to a worthless pair of flip-flops, it may seem harmless to let your dog have the ruined shoes as a toy. You might even imagine that having an object of yours will be a comfort to him when you are away. Unfortunately, this is all wishful thinking. By tolerating further destruction—even if you can no longer use the item—you are making it nearly impossible for your dog to discern "fair-game" objects from those that are off limits. Your English Cocker won't know the difference between the sneakers he has inherited and the brand-new pair you buy next week to replace them.

This isn't to say that English Cocker Spaniels aren't intelligent dogs. On the contrary! English Cockers are smart animals who enjoy toys and games that challenge them both physically and mentally. When shopping for toys, look for items that involve some problem-solving, such as balls that hold and release a special treat when rolled the right way. (These work especially well for dogs who will be spending time alone each day.) English Cockers also love to play fetch and hide-and-seek. The possibilities are endless.

You will likely find your dog is even capable of teaching you some new games along the way. You may buy a toy with one

Identify Your Pet

Get your English Cocker a personalized ID tag engraved with his name, as well as your name, address, and phone number.

purpose in mind, but not realize its full potential until your English Cocker shows you what can really be done with it. My first American Cocker Spaniel, Jonathan, taught me a game I dubbed the "Russian Spy" game. He would shake and torture his stuffed suspects until they gave up the world-saving information that he sought from them. Some would squeal at the first sign of pressure, while others would tough it out through loss of eyes and limbs.

Okay, so I did a little inventing of my own, but that's the idea: Have fun with it, and your dog will, too.

Tags

When I think of dog licenses, I am always reminded of that precious scene from Disney's in which Lady receives her shiny new license, and how proud she is to wear it on her collar. When you license your English Cocker Spaniel, you should be proud, too, as the revenue collected from dog licenses in most counties helps pay for investigations into animal cruelty complaints, enforcement of animal welfare laws, and care for sick or injured stray animals.

Most states require dog owners to license their pets. Although it might be tempting to skip this seemingly insignificant step, keep in mind that the number on your pet's license tag serves as legal identification if your dog should ever become lost. The fee for registration is usually minimal—even less for a spayed or neutered dog—but you will need to renew the registration annually. Keep the tag affixed to your dog's collar or harness at all times; remember, a tag number can only serve as identification if your dog wears the tag!

When applying for a dog license, you will likely need to provide a valid rabies vaccination certificate and proof of spaying or neutering, if applicable. Requirements vary from one area to another, though, so call your local city or town offices to see what documents are necessary in your area and where licenses may be purchased.

As an added safety measure, many owners also invest in a separate identification tag. Unlike your dog's license, which only displays a number, this personalized tag may be engraved with detailed information such as your dog's name as well as your name, address, and phone number. Most pet supply retailers now have self-serve machines that engrave these inexpensive custom tags within minutes. You can also purchase them through catalogs or online. Be sure the information on your dog's tag is always up to date, and don't forget to include all the necessary details.

Although some collars are affixed with labels for identification purposes, the written information can fade over time, so an engraved tag is a more reliable choice.

Microchipping & Tattooing

If you remove your English Cocker's collar when inside the house for safety reasons, and your dog manages to get outside and escape, the registration tag left behind obviously can't help with identification. Additionally, if your dog is ever stolen, even a reasonably intelligent

Provide your English Cocker with chews and toys that are suitable for his size and chewing power.

thief will remove any identification tags immediately. Taking photographs of your dog (particularly ones that capture any distinguishing marks) is a wise precaution, and it may provide authorities with a valuable means of finding your dog in the event that he is ever lost or taken from you. Even photos, however, cannot prove ownership conclusively. For this reason, it is wise to provide your dog with a permanent form of identification. There are two main methods, microchipping and tattooing—neither of which will disqualify or count against a dog in the show ring.

One of the most efficient forms of permanent animal identification is microchipping. Performed by a veterinarian, this innovative process consists of implanting a tiny electronic device (approximately the size of a grain of rice) beneath the skin between your English Cocker's shoulder blades. The entire procedure is as quick and painless as a vaccination. In the event that your dog is lost or stolen, the chip may then be scanned with a handheld device at virtually any shelter or veterinary hospital.

Tattooing is another common means of animal identification, but one that is somewhat waning in popularity since the widespread availability of the microchip. Most commonly applied to the inside of the right thigh, a canine tattoo is applied in a similar manner as a human's. A unique number in permanent ink is applied

Basic Items Every New Cocker Owner Needs

Of course, your list of supplies will gradually expand once your new English Cocker Spaniel arrives home, but the following items will help you set up house for those first few weeks:

- Brush and nail clippers
- Collar and leash
- Crate and liner
- Food and water bowls
- Odor-absorbing cleaner
- Puppy food
- Puppy shampoo
- Safe, chewable toys

with a needle onto the dog's skin. Because the process can be painful, though, an animal must be under sedation for the entire procedure—an added expense and an unnecessary risk if there is no other reason for the animal to be under the anesthesia. (If you decide to have your English Cocker tattooed, consider doing so when he goes under anesthesia to be spayed or neutered.) Also, the permanence of tattooing as a means of identification is often disputed, as anyone with experience in this field can alter a tattoo relatively easily. Although vets and shelters will check a dog for both a microchip and a tattoo, a microchip is more likely to help return a dog to his rightful owner.

If you decide to safeguard your English Cocker with either a microchip or a tattoo, it is vital that you register your dog's number with the appropriate agency. The agency's directory will link your dog to you. You must also be sure to update your contact information whenever it changes. Also, if you move to a new community, let your new vet know that your dog has been microchipped or tattooed so that she can add the information to your dog's records at the new hospital.

If you wish to have one of these procedures done, ask your vet about it as soon as possible. Once your dog is lost or stolen, it will be too late.

FINDING YOUR ENGLISH COCKER'S HOME AWAY FROM HOME

Dog Daycare and Pet Sitters

As long as your English Cocker Spaniel is provided with a chance to relieve himself and get a little exercise about halfway through the day, leaving your dog alone while you work shouldn't be a problem. Although we may like to think our dogs need our constant attention, an English Cocker will do just fine with an owner who is employed full time, provided there isn't a considerable amount of overtime involved.

If you have a demanding job that calls for many hours away from home, and you also want an English Cocker Spaniel, a bit more planning will be necessary. No, this doesn't mean taking your dog to work with you (although that is certainly a fantastic option if possible). By utilizing a professional pet sitter or a dog daycare, you can make your busy schedule work for both you and your dog.

Dog daycares, similar to children's daycare facilities, are now available in most areas to help people just like you make sure that their dogs are getting enough attention, exercise, and mental stimulation during the workday. Dogs in these facilities are typically divided into groups according to size and temperament and allowed to take part in a number of scheduled activities throughout the day, including walks, games, and free play periods.

Choosing a Dog Daycare

When choosing a daycare, be sure to take a tour of the premises. Ask the director as many questions as possible, and observe the environment carefully. How friendly is the staff? Are there a sufficient number of caregivers for all the dogs? Are the facilities clean?

Employees should have experience dealing with dogs and possess an obvious rapport with animals. The ratio of staff members to dogs may vary, but employees who seem frazzled are likely an indication that there aren't enough people to properly manage all the dogs. A practical ratio is at least 1 employee for every 10 dogs.

Cleanliness is also extremely important. Since diseases can easily be passed through canine urine and fecal matter, any accidents should be cleaned immediately and thoroughly. A faint smell of

bleach is a good sign that the facilities are kept clean and hygienic. You should also ask to see the area where the dogs are taken to relieve themselves and make sure this is also reasonably clean and well maintained.

Ask the director to describe the different organized activities that the facility offers. Find out which other breeds are usually grouped with English Cockers and how many dogs are allowed to participate in recreation at once. You will also want to confirm that all interactions are supervised and ask how squabbles between dogs are handled when they arise. Voice reprimands and time-out rooms are both humane and effective discipline methods, but never leave your dog at a facility that allows any form of physical punishment.

Identifying your dog properly makes it much more likely that he will be returned to you should he become lost.

Ask about the criteria for admission. All dogs should be evaluated to determine the group in which they will be placed. Important factors in this assessment should include a dog's breed, size, and temperament.

Also, ask about emergency protocol. Is there a veterinarian on the premises? If not, are employees trained in canine cardiopulmonary resuscitation (CPR) and first aid? Which veterinary hospital will be used in the event of a serious injury or other medical crisis? How and when will you be notified?

You will be required to provide a copy of your English Cocker's immunization record before he is accepted

into a program. The list of necessary vaccinations may vary from business to business, but will likely include rabies, DHLP-P (distemper/parvo combination), and Bordetella (kennel cough). The Bordetella vaccine may be new to you, but it is especially important since your English Cocker will be in the presence of so many other dogs. For this same reason, there may be a mandatory test for intestinal parasites. Additionally, your dog may be required to be spayed or neutered. While they may seem stringent, these prerequisites help ensure a safe and healthy environment for all the animals involved.

You don't need to work long hours to employ daycare. This can be a productive choice even for owners who only work part time. If your dog doesn't often get the opportunity to be around other dogs or people, being part of this kind of community can help build valuable social skills that will come in especially handy if you plan to involve him in any advanced training activities or if you plan to add another dog to your household down the road. Having regular contact with humans other than his owner will only make an English Cocker friendlier, and it can even ease the pain of separation anxiety, a common behavioral problem among dogs.

If your English Cocker isn't accepted into daycare, don't assume something is wrong with him or that you have done something wrong to cause the problem. Just like people, dogs can have very different personalities, and some dogs are simply not cut out for this kind of environment. Consider hiring a professional pet sitter or dog walker if this is the case.

Choosing a Pet Sitter

Pet sitters can be hired to come to your home and stay with your dog for a predetermined amount of time. Your veterinarian or local animal shelter should be able to recommend someone in your area who offers this kind of service. You might even have a friend or neighbor who would be interested in the job. In many ways, having a pet sitter is even better than using daycare, since so much more individual attention is involved.

If getting home to walk your English Cocker Spaniel in the middle of the day is your biggest challenge, a dog walker may be the best alternative. Like a pet sitter, a dog walker will come to your home and give your dog a chance to stretch his legs and relieve himself so that you don't have to make an extra commute every day on your lunch hour.

Costs can vary depending on demand in your area, but remember that, in most cases, you get what you pay for. Whether you are placing your dog in daycare or having someone come to your home while you are away, interview potential candidates for the job thoroughly. Ask for references, and always check them. Even more importantly, if you get a bad feeling, continue your search. In the case of a sitter or dog walker, this person will need keys to your home—an awesome responsibility. In any of these situations, though, you will be entrusting the person you choose with something completely irreplaceable: your beloved English Cocker Spaniel.

Boarding

If you plan to travel without bringing your dog along, you will need to make arrangements in advance for his care while you are gone. If you take only occasional trips, you may have a friend or neighbor who will take care of your English Cocker while you are away. If this is not an option, or you go out of town frequently, look into boarding kennels.

As the name implies, a boarding kennel provides your dog with food and lodging when you will be away from home overnight or longer. Although you won't be using a kennel's services as often as you might use a daycare's, it is equally important that you select a trustworthy establishment. Again, your veterinarian or local animal shelter should be able to provide you with a list of reputable businesses of this kind in your area. Some veterinarians even offer boarding services for their clients right on the hospital's premises. Recommendations from your breeder or other dog-owning friends can also be helpful.

Just like a daycare, a boarding kennel will have a list of health requirements and will ask you to provide proof that your dog meets these requirements before granting him boarding privileges. Even if you won't be traveling for a while, you should start looking into kennels as soon as possible if you plan to use one, and follow up on any necessary vaccinations or tests your dog may need right away. If you wait until the last minute, your vet's appointment calendar might be heavily booked, and you could find yourself without a place for your dog during your trip.

Always schedule your boarding reservations well in advance, also, as each kennel can only accommodate so many animals at one time. Some businesses may be booked up for weeks or even months before major holidays and other popular vacation times.

Choosing a Boarding Facility

You will use many of the same criteria in evaluating a boarding service as you would a daycare. The facilities should be clean, pens should be of adequate size, and the employees should be knowledgeable and friendly, with a penchant for animals. Although the primary objective of a kennel isn't to entertain your dog, daily exercise should be provided. A boarding service that meets all these standards and also offers some fun activities for your dog is ideal. Costs, again, can vary by region, but you will generally pay less per day for boarding than daycare, since a large staff generally isn't necessary for boarding.

When leaving your dog at the kennel, a quick goodbye will help make the experience easier for all involved. English Cockers are excellent at picking up on apprehension. To help ensure that your dog is as comfortable as possible during his stay, though, ask in advance if you may bring along his bed, food, and toys. Having these familiar items can be especially soothing for a dog.

Time and Attention

Of course, daycare is not a substitute for an owner's one-on-one attention. If you have an English Cocker, you must have time to spend with him. It doesn't matter what you do together. Whether you are tossing around a squeak toy, competing in agility, or indulging your pet with a relaxing belly rub nothing is more precious to an English Cocker Spaniel than time with his owner.

Before boarding your dog, visit the facility to make sure you will be comfortable leaving your pet there.

Chapter

4

FEEDING
Your English Cocker Spaniel

At one time, feeding the family dog meant picking up a bag of kibble at the grocery store and serving it up alongside a few table scraps. Some owners opted for canned food instead, but purchased it from that same grocery store. The brand may have been chosen due to a shrewd marketing campaign touting the food's exaggerated benefits— usually ingredients such as vegetables, grains, and meats. Or maybe it was just the cheapest option. No one gave much thought to issues like byproducts, common food allergens, or the dangers posed by unhealthy preservatives. Fortunately, as we educated ourselves about our own nutrition, we also began to learn more about our dog's diets, and how improving them could help our pets lead longer, healthier lives.

The result has been a vast selection of feeding options for your English Cocker Spaniel, a virtual cornucopia of prepackaged, home-cooked, and even raw foods that all claim to best serve your dog's nutritional needs. So, how do you decide which approach is best for your dog? Like popular human diets, most canine food plans have both advantages and disadvantages. Deciding which one is right for your dog can largely depend on his individual needs.

WHAT TO FEED YOUR ENGLISH COCKER

Prepackaged Food

Prepackaged dog food has evolved from a product of convenience into an effective means of providing some of the very best canine nutrition on the market today. While brands containing potentially harmful byproducts and preservatives still fill the shelves along with their healthier counterparts, a little research can yield a whole lot of peace of mind. Armed with just a few pieces of key information about what ingredients are best, it usually won't take long to differentiate the healthiest options from the less desirable choices.

Check the labels of any commercial foods you offer your English Cocker to ensure they are nutritious and of high quality.

Read the Label

When selecting a prepackaged dog food, do the same thing you would do if you were shopping for your human family members—read those labels! Just as you would inspect the food label for a human food, look for the ingredients list on the back of a dog food package. By law, the packages must list the food's ingredients in descending order by weight. In other words, the most prevalent ingredient should be listed first. If the first ingredient is chicken byproducts, for instance, the largest part of the food includes things like chicken beaks and feet—items not considered fit by the US Food and Drug Administration (FDA) for human consumption. This would be the first red flag that this may not be the best food for your English Cocker.

Sometimes, however, the job of discerning the best foods from the less desirable ones requires a bit more scrutiny. For example, some manufacturers have found a crafty way around this law by splitting inferior ingredients into separate categories. This makes it possible for them to push the food's better ingredients toward the top of the list even though the substandard ingredients predominantly outweigh them. A common practice is listing several different types of grain individually so that the food appears to be chicken-based when in actuality it is grain-based.

In addition to byproducts, another ingredient you may want to avoid is bone meal—meat and bones that are ground up with most of the water removed. Meal serves as an inexpensive source of protein for dog food companies, but it is far less efficient for your English Cocker Spaniel. Both meat and poultry byproduct meal contain parts of animals not normally eaten by people, and meal containing large amounts of bone will be difficult for your dog to digest, as well as deficient in nutritional value.

Preservatives

Preservatives can be an especially tricky area. While any food that isn't eaten almost immediately needs some type of preservative to keep it fresh, some are thought to be considerably safer than others. Since the average 25-pound (11.3 kg) dog consumes between 6 and 9 pounds (2.7 and 4.1 kg) of chemical preservatives each year, careful selection of preservatives is a must.

Preservatives to avoid include synthetic preservatives such as butylated hydroxyanisole (BHA), butylated hydroxytoluene (BHT), and ethoxyquin. These have all come under particular scrutiny in recent years. Studies have shown that very high levels of BHA can cause tumors in the forestomachs of rats, mice, and hamsters. However, since no data have been collected relating to animals lacking a forestomach, and dog foods contain such a minute percentage (0.02 percent of the fat content only), these preservatives are still allowed in dog foods in low amounts. Although reliable data on ethoxyquin have been limited, there has been sufficient concern for the FDA's Center for Veterinary Medicine to request that dog food companies significantly lower the levels of ethoxyquin in their products.

Among the better preservatives are tocopherols, vitamin-based preservatives used in some canine food brands. Unfortunately, foods that include these healthier preservatives have a shorter shelf life (especially once a package has been opened), but this is an area in which your dog's health should take precedence over the convenience of being able to buy in bulk. I like to think of making more frequent trips to the pet supply store as an excuse to take my own dogs out for regular outings.

Do Your Research

Look for the manufacturer's phone number when reading a pet food label. Although companies are only legally required to print their names and addresses on the packages, customers should be able to call with any questions they may have. Many dog food companies also list extensive nutritional information (including customer service e-mail addresses) on their websites.

Dry, Wet, or Semi-moist?

If, like most dog owners, you have decided to feed your English Cocker Spaniel a prepackaged food, you will then be confronted with a variety of choices among different formulas, consistencies, and even bite sizes. Some selections should be based on your dog's age, weight, and general health. Others may depend on what works best for your lifestyle.

First, you will need to decide if you want to feed your dog dry (often called kibble), wet, or semi-moist food. Kibble is usually the most cost effective of the three, and unlike wet food, it can sit uneaten in a bowl all day long without spoiling. It is important to note that dogs on dry diets generally require more water than dogs eating wet food, so be sure to make water a priority if going this route. Dry food also tends to produce consistently solid stools, an important factor for many owners. Wet foods can be more appealing to a picky eater, but dogs on wet diets need more meticulous dental care, since plaque and tartar form more quickly on their teeth.

Semi-moist foods might appear to be a good compromise between the two, but because they contain a large amount of sugar, most are less than ideal. A high sugar intake is associated with many canine health problems, including diabetes and obesity. If you prefer feeding a softer food without all the wetness of canned varieties, consider dog food rolls. These foods are packaged similarly to salamis and frequently offer a combination of good nutrition and an impressive shelf life. Do check those labels, though, just as you would for any other kind of food. The best brands will contain no byproducts.

Choosing a Formula

After you have settled on the consistency of your dog's food, you will then need to select a specific formula. In addition to age-based formulas, high-energy, weight-maintenance, and several other kinds of foods are available. If your dog has joint problems, you may choose a food made for arthritic dogs. If your dog is physically active, a high-energy formula may be best. I feed my own Cockers a mixture of a lamb and rice adult formula and the dental-friendly variety of the same brand. I simply buy a small bag

An enormous variety of commercial dog foods is available in dry, wet, or semi-moist forms.

of each and mix them together before feeding. I find this works better than swapping between the two, as even minor changes in diet can disrupt dogs' bowels.

Keeping It Fresh

No matter which food you choose for your dog, it is vitally important that you keep it as fresh as possible. Canned food should be refrigerated immediately after opening, but dry food also needs to be carefully contained to ensure freshness. If you store dry food in anything other than its original bag (I use a small bin), be sure to wash the container whenever you add new food. Fat from the older food can settle to the bottom and spoil, contaminating the fresh food and possibly making your pet sick. Also, whatever the container, make sure it is tightly sealed when stored.

Home Cooking

For some dog owners, the easiest way to make sure their pets are getting the exact amount of the nutrients they need without any byproducts or chemicals is by feeding their dogs fresh foods prepared through good old-fashioned home-cooking. If you regularly cook healthy meals for your other family members, cooking for just one more may not be much of a chore for you, and the benefits could be numerous. When done correctly, a home-cooked canine diet can be a wonderful asset to your dog's health and also a great combatant against the biggest downside to prepackaged foods—monotony! Like human diets, home-cooked canine meals can offer a great variety of tasty foods. Home-cooking can be rather expensive and time-consuming, though, so consider all sides before committing to an exclusively home-cooked plan.

Feeding Healthy Foods

Like people, dogs need a healthful mix of meats, grains, and vegetables in their diets. Broccoli, carrots, and leafy greens are wonderful staples for a canine diet. Raw fruits served sliced make a nice addition when offered occasionally. Rice is a very common ingredient in many home-cooked canine diets, since it has been shown to help manage many canine digestive problems. Meat, fish, and eggs are all excellent sources of protein, but don't feed eggs (either raw or cooked) too frequently since they are so high in cholesterol—try to limit them to just a couple each week. Although

Water— The Unsung Nutrient

Water is one of the most undervalued nutrients in both animals and humans. Just a 10-percent loss of your Cocker's total body water can lead to serious illness; a loss of 15 percent of more will cause death. Water is the primary vehicle for transporting nutrients throughout your dog's body and for removing wastes from his system in the form of urine. It helps with digestion and circulation and is also responsible for regulating your dog's body temperature. Moreover, whatever amount of water your dog loses throughout the day, he needs to consume an equal amount for replacement. Fresh water must always be available to your English Cocker Spaniel—not only at mealtime, but at all other times, as well.

Offering home-cooked meals can have great benefits for your English Cocker, but home-cooked diets are more expensive and time-consuming than prepackaged foods.

cottage cheese and yogurt can add valuable calcium to your dog's diet without causing any major digestive issues, try to limit other dairy products as these can be highly indigestible for dogs.

Educate yourself not only about healthy foods, but also about those that are harmful to dogs, such as chocolate and onions. Never offer your dog any food containing these ingredients, and remember that this off-limits list includes cocoa and onion powder, too. Also, refrain from seasoning your dog's food with salt. Most dogs are not nearly as finicky as our human family members can be and likely won't care whether their food is seasoned or not.

Even if you feel certain that you have all of your dog's nutritional bases covered, it is wise to consult your veterinarian before beginning this new feeding regimen so that you are sure not to overlook anything. Your vet can identify any deficiencies in your plan and the best ways to compensate for them. She may also be able to point you toward valuable resources for this endeavor, such as the best books on the topic of canine home-cooking and even possible menus for meal planning.

Raw Food

Like the proponents of other kinds of canine diets, supporters of the BARF diet (an acronym standing for "bones and raw food") feel strongly that their nutritional plan is best. The premise is simple: raw foods retain natural enzymes and antioxidants that are destroyed by the heat processing of prepared foods. English Cockers placed on raw diets consume raw vegetables, raw eggs, and dairy foods in addition to raw meats and bones.

While there are many benefits to this method of feeding, including shinier coats, cleaner teeth, and better overall health quality according to its devotees, there are also some very real liabilities. The risks of choking or becoming internally injured by bones can in fact be deadly. Chicken bones, with their small size and tendency to splinter, are particularly dangerous.

Feeding raw foods can be less expensive than buying prepackaged foods, since owners can plan their dogs' menus based on the weekly grocery sales. With all its advantages, though, the BARF diet is not suitable for most smaller dog breeds, which are at an increased risk for internal injuries. Bones can also cause broken teeth, which can make eating difficult and painful for the rest of your Cocker's life.

WHEN TO FEED YOUR ENGLISH COCKER

In addition to all the other decisions you must make regarding your English Cocker Spaniel's diet, you also have to decide whether to schedule your dog's meals or opt for free feeding (leaving food available at all times) instead. Both choices offer specific benefits and liabilities.

Free Feeding

If your dog has a hard time knowing when to say "when," free feeding can lead to obesity. However, eating several smaller meals throughout the day is a healthier option than two larger ones, if your dog can handle the innate freedom of having food available all the time.

You may also favor the ease of free feeding, since you will simply need to clean your dog's dishes once a day and make sure they are filled with fresh food and water when convenient. Bear in mind, though, that it may well be difficult to housetrain a puppy who is eating as much as he wants whenever he wants. Until the housetraining phase concludes, it may be wise to postpone free feeding for this reason.

If you do opt for free feeding, never merely top off your dog's food and water. Even when food is made available at all times, your English Cocker Spaniel's dishes should be cleaned thoroughly every day. Harmful germs and bacteria quickly build up on dishes that are left unwashed; if your dog is eating from dirty bowls, he is also ingesting those germs along with his food. A handy tip for easy feeding is to purchase two sets of dishes for your dog. By going this route, you should always have a clean set of bowls

A Little of Both

If you like the idea of feeding your dog home-cooked meals, but you simply do not have the time for this considerable undertaking, consider enhancing your dog's current prepackaged food with just a small amount of home-cooked fare. Likewise, you can always supplement a home-cooked diet with a sensible amount of quality kibble. By feeding your dog both home-cooked and prepackaged foods, you can conveniently offer him both the variety and balanced nutrition he deserves.

ready, even as the dirty set heads into the dishwasher.

Scheduled Feeding

Scheduled feeding tends to work better for owners who board their English Cocker Spaniels or leave them with friends while traveling. It is also more practical for dogs who participate in daycare programs. Whenever someone else cares for your dog, schedules can be very helpful, but they cannot be implemented at the last minute. A dog who is accustomed to eating whenever he likes will not automatically adapt to receiving scheduled meals. Whatever feeding style you choose, it is important that it be consistent.

If you wish to change your English Cocker Spaniel from a free-feeding routine to structured feeding times, it can be done, but it will likely take some time and effort. Even if you would ultimately like to offer your Cocker just two meals a day, begin by dividing his food into four or five meals. Once he adjusts to this change, you may then decrease the number gradually until the transition is complete.

When making this transition, it is especially important that you limit treats and other foods, because you want your dog to eat at his meal times. If he gorges on snacks at other times, he will likely eat less of his meal when the time comes, and he will almost certainly be hungry at a non-feeding time later. If you try changing him over too rapidly (with or without occasional treats), your Cocker may refuse to eat his food at the new times and could subsequently suffer a seizure from hypoglycemia (low blood sugar).

If the advantages of feeding several smaller meals each day appeal to you, but you don't think free feeding is a constructive choice for your dog, there is a third option. Simply divide the amount of food your Cocker is currently eating among a greater number of meals, as eating more can negate the benefits of this regimen.

A LIFETIME OF GOOD NUTRITION

As human beings grow and age, their dietary needs change along with them; the same is true for dogs. Most owners realize that puppies require diets formulated especially for their growing

Decide whether you want to offer your English Cocker scheduled meals or provide food throughout the day. Both methods have their own advantages and disadvantages.

bodies, but not everyone knows about the importance of tailoring a canine diet to other age groups and metabolisms. Assuming that the only change you will need to make to your English Cocker Spaniel's diet will be the transition from puppy to adult food can limit his nutrition and affect his health dramatically.

Puppies

When English Cocker Spaniel puppies are born, they usually nurse each time they awaken. My own breeder has told me that even when her pups have just eaten and fallen into slumber, when the mom wakes them up to clean them, they will eat once again before drifting back off to sleep. Although your weaned puppy won't need to eat quite this often, he will need to load up on his nutrients more often than an adult English Cocker, as puppies need nearly twice the amount of energy of full-grown dogs. (Puppies have very high metabolisms and also need more protein and calories to grow properly.)

Although some veterinarians still stand by the old rule of transitioning all puppies to adult food when they turn a year old (no matter what their breed), many vets and English Cocker Spaniel breeders now recommend making the switch a bit sooner than this. The reason for this is that smaller breeds tend to reach their adult weight long before the full one-year mark. To prevent overgrowth, which can result in a number of health conditions

A Family That Eats Together . . .

A funny thing seems to happen to many owners who choose free feeding—their dogs prefer to eat when the rest of the family eats. Coincidence? Probably not. Like most people, dogs truly enjoy the company of their family members and want to be a part of their daily routine.

Whether you free feed or schedule your English Cocker Spaniel's meals, make a point to place his dishes in the room in which you eat your own meals. Just as you enjoy sitting around the dinner table discussing the day's events, your dog will enjoy spending this time with the people he loves most—nourishing both his body and soul.

including arthritis and hip dysplasia, start feeding your English Cocker pup adult food somewhere between the ages of 4 and 10 months, depending on his individual size and overall proportion. If your dog has reached his adult size by six months, for example, it may be time to consider making the switch.

Making the Switch

When you are ready to start feeding adult food, remember the importance of making a gradual change. As with any move from one type of food to another, it is vital that you introduce only a small percentage of the new food at a time. Begin with only 25 percent, waiting to increase this ratio until your dog seems to have acclimated to the initial change. About a week later, you should be able to move to a 50 percent mix, then 75 percent the week after that, and so on. You do not necessarily have to make changes weekly, though. The full transition can take weeks or even months, but you should always wait at least a week or so before increasing the amount of new food. An abrupt change in your Cocker's digestive system can lead to unpleasant gastrointestinal issues, such as stomach upset and diarrhea.

Adult Dogs

The dietary needs of adult dogs can vary as much as the dogs themselves. Whether your English Cocker Spaniel competes in agility or accompanies you for your daily run, your active dog will need a diet formulated specifically for high-energy animals. Conversely, if your English Cocker has spent too much time playing couch potato, he may likely need to be temporarily placed on a weight-reduction formula. Or perhaps your dog's teeth seem especially prone to calculus (tartar), in which case a tartar-control formula may be best for him.

Your dog's weight can be an excellent barometer for diet planning. Just as you need to make adjustments if your dog starts to gain weight, you also need to make changes if your dog is underweight. Your veterinarian should be able to tell you for sure if your dog falls within the acceptable weight range for his height and bone structure. (Yep, just like people, English Cockers can be either small- or large-boned.) A good test to conduct on your own, to see if your dog's weight is a problem, is to feel his midsection. Ideally, your Cocker's ribs should be discernible, but not obvious. There should be a thin layer of fat over this area that is easily penetrated by gentle touch. When looking down at your dog, you should be able to make out his waist, but it should not be prominent.

Since a dog's metabolism can change repeatedly during his adult years, you should perform this test periodically to make sure you are feeding your dog the right amount of food. A two-year-old English Cocker who chases tennis balls daily can burn calories at a very different rate than a six-year-old dog with similar exercise

Your dog should always have access to clean, fresh water.

Sample Feeding Schedule for the Different Phases of Your Cocker's Life

PUPPIES LESS THAN FOUR MONTHS	PUPPIES BETWEEN FOUR MONTHS AND ONE YEAR	ADULT DOGS	SENIOR DOGS
English Cocker Spaniel puppies need three meals per day: in the morning, at midday, and in the early evening. Water should be offered with each meal and then once more a short time after the last meal of the day. While housetraining, be sure to remove your puppy's water bowl one to two hours before bedtime.	Around the time older puppies are transitioned to adult food, they should also be switched to just two meals per day — eliminating the midday meal. Once housetraining is mastered, water can be offered at all times. Watch your dog for excessive drinking, though, as this might be a sign of a medical problem.	Adult dogs should also be fed two meals per day, but variety can be added by offering a mix of wet and dry food or some raw vegetables to either meal. Since dogs' metabolisms slow as they get older, stick to only healthy treats and swap to a weight-reduction diet if your dog becomes overweight.	Dogs sometimes lose their zest for eating as they age. Try offering several smaller meals each day or warming up your dog's wet food to make eating more fun. Since raw vegetables may be more difficult for your older dog to chew, try offering softer treats like cottage cheese or an occasional hard-boiled egg instead.

habits. It is far easier to deal with a weight gain before it adds up to several pounds.

If you suddenly begin taking your Cocker along on lengthy hikes, however, you may need to increase the amount of calories in his diet to provide him with sufficient energy for the activity. While an active dog can certainly be given more treats than an obese one, you mustn't try to depend on treats for all your dog's additional caloric needs. Depending on the intensity of the exercise, you should either increase the amount of his current food (be careful, though; just a little more food can go a long way) or start feeding a high-energy formula.

Knowing which pet food formula is best for your English Cocker Spaniel can seem overwhelming, especially when you are standing in the pet supply store amid your numerous options. You may even end up trying several different kinds before settling on a diet that ultimately fits your dog's needs best. Rest assured, no single formula is right for every dog—or even every Cocker. If you have any questions about whether your dog is getting the proper amount of nutrition, talk to your veterinarian.

Aging Adults and Seniors

As your English Cocker Spaniel gets older, his diet will again need to be adjusted for optimum health. A slowing metabolism, the aches and pains associated with aging, and even an indifference to the food he once loved can all present new challenges for you and your mature dog. By fortifying your dog's diet with the proper balance of nutrients for an aging animal, however, you can help your English Cocker rise to the challenge of growing older.

When does your Cocker become a senior, though? Obviously, your dog will not wake up one morning and suddenly step through the threshold to his golden years. The exact age that dogs move from adulthood to senior status differs from breed to breed—and even from dog to dog. Generally, though, most dogs are considered older when they enter the last third of their projected life expectancy. For English Cocker Spaniels, this is around the age of 10.

Feeding Tips

Dogs would eat steak and eggs at every meal if given the choice—and most of a dog's protein does come from meat and eggs. Fido, however, needs a complete, balanced diet. Cheese and milk are great sources of protein, although many dogs are sensitive to lactose products. Many premium dog foods provide a nutritionally balanced meal, so settling on one brand may boil down to what a pooch most enjoys. The ideal dog food is a low-fat, high-fiber one.

(Courtesy of the AAHA and Healthypet.com)

What to Feed a Senior Dog

Like puppies, older dogs need a greater amount of protein in their diets. This can be accomplished by selecting a high-quality prepackaged food formulated especially for senior dogs. You can also increase the amount of protein in a raw or home-cooked regimen by feeding a higher percentage of foods such as chicken, fish, and eggs. Senior diets should also include less fat and fewer calories than adult regimens.

Most prepackaged senior diets also include a small amount of such supplements as glucosamine and chondroitin, which can be helpful in dealing with conditions like arthritis and other joint problems. Usually, though, this is just a negligible amount, so talk to your veterinarian about incorporating an additional quantity of these supplements into your English Cocker's diet. Although you can certainly hide them in food as you would other pills, many people simply open the capsules and sprinkle the contents over their dogs' food.

Although the transition to a senior food might seem like it would be the last major change to your Cocker's diet, many dogs will require additional changes due to certain health issues. If your dog experiences diabetes, renal (kidney) problems, or another serious condition, you may need to make yet another dietary change. You may also need to make some minor changes if your dog loses a significant number of teeth from decay or extraction. This could mean merely feeding a smaller kibble, changing the consistency of your dog's current food with a blender, or changing to an entirely different kind of food.

SUPPLEMENTATION AND SPECIAL DIETS

If you read up on human nutrition, you will quickly learn that many experts recommend preparing vegetables *al dente*—heated or steamed to the point of being firm, but not soft. By overcooking many vegetables, many people reduce their food's vitamin content significantly. A similar thing can happen to the vitamins and minerals in your dog's prepackaged food due to the heat and pressure of manufacturing. For this and other reasons, many veterinarians now recommend giving dogs dietary supplements to help make up for these deficiencies.

Supplements can also help with various health problems, as well as cosmetic ones. Vitamin E, for example, can improve coat quality.

Talk to your vet before adding any dietary supplements to your pet's diet.

Together, vitamins C and D help make collagen, which strengthens tendons and ligaments. B-complex vitamins help maintain nerve function. Often touted for their healing properties, wheat grass and spirulina have also become extremely popular in the canine supplement community.

It is vital to note that just because a substance is considered natural, this does not necessarily mean that the element is safe for your dog. Some supplements, while completely safe for humans, are not appropriate for animals. Dosages can also vary depending on a dog's age, breed, and other factors. For safety's sake, never give your dog *any* supplement without prior approval from your veterinarian.

Another way to treat certain medical conditions is to feed a special diet. Your veterinarian may suggest either a temporary or permanent change to one of these prescription regimens as a means of managing allergies, a gastrointestinal condition, or even kidney problems. Commonly, feeding a bland diet of lamb and rice (sometimes with cottage cheese) is recommended instead, although this is usually only a temporary measure.

DEALING WITH FOOD-RELATED PROBLEMS

Getting a Handle on Treats

In addition to considering what your adult dog should be eating, it is just as important to watch out for things he *shouldn't* be eating. As long as your English Cocker isn't overweight, there is nothing wrong with offering him treats, providing they are not nutritionally deficient or excessive in either quantity or frequency. Even healthy snacks must be consumed in moderation to avoid unnecessary weight gain. A great trick for keeping your dog's weight under control while still allowing sensible treats is breaking a dog biscuit (or any other kind of treat) in half before giving it to your dog. You can break them up either one at a time as needed or all at once if you transfer your dog's treats from their package to a special container.

As tempting as it may be to share "junk food" with your English Cocker, snacks like potato chips and cookies are just as unhealthy for your canine buddy as they are for you—even more so when you consider your Cocker's size in proportion to your own. What

Ways to Rejuvinate an Aging Appetite

Add some of the water from a tuna fish can or low-fat, low-salt chicken broth to your dog's food. Both the scent and taste may make his ho-hum kibble more enticing. As long as your dog is fit and healthy, you may also occasionally use meat drippings, clam juice, and even meat itself. Variety, in fact, can be a huge motivator for a finicky senior.

Another great way to utilize powerful smells is by simply bringing out the natural aromas of your dog's food by heating it before serving. This works best with wet or home-cooked food, but you can also add a little water to dry kibble before warming it up. When you consider how pleasing eating a cold meal night after night would be for you, it is easy to see how this simple step can help restore your dog's interest in eating. Do be careful, though, when heating your dog's food (particularly in a microwave) so that it doesn't get too hot. A good way to check is to place your finger in the middle of the bowl after stirring the contents.

Canned food is often more appealing to dogs than dry. Although we only feed it occasionally in our house, our Cockers always come running at the first sound of the can opener. If you feed your older dog canned food consistently, look for a weight-maintenance formula to ensure that you don't better his appetite by sacrificing his healthy weight.

may seem like innocent indulgences can place your beloved pet on the road to serious illness. Although it may take years for saturated fats and sugar to infiltrate your own arteries, your dog's smaller body will succumb to conditions such as heart disease and diabetes significantly faster than yours.

Obesity

As a country that is predominantly overweight, we are sadly passing our bad habits of overeating and underexercising on to not only our children, but also our pets. It is important to understand that allowing your English Cocker Spaniel to become obese is one of the most serious forms of neglect. While it may not be as blatant or even as intentional as striking an animal or refusing to feed him at all, overfeeding can ultimately hurt your dog just as much as these other behaviors. If your dog is overweight, the time to work on this problem is now.

How to Tell If Your English Cocker Is Overweight

The healthy weights of different dogs will vary depending on such factors as gender, genetics, and activity level. What is most important is that your adult English Cocker Spaniel maintains the weight that is most healthy for him. In addition to a higher number on the scale, signs that your dog has gained too much weight may include waddling when walking, shortness of breath after minimal exercise, and your not being able to easily feel his ribs.

Diet and Exercise

The first and most obvious step in helping your dog lose excess weight is lowering both the calories and fat content of his food. First, check to see if you have been feeding your dog the right amount of food for his age and size. If your dog is only slightly overweight, cutting back to the recommended serving size may be enough to solve the problem. If he is significantly overweight, though, a weight-reduction diet may likely be necessary.

If you have only been giving your dog the amount indicated for his particular food, and he has nonetheless begun to gain weight, another issue may be present, such as a thyroid disorder. If this is the case, it is especially important to talk to your vet before placing your dog on a new diet or implementing a new exercise program.

Even if your dog appears completely healthy, it is wise to contact your vet before any major dietary cutback or increase in exercise. If your English Cocker has never exercised past the point of simple play, he will need to make the move toward more intense physical activity gradually. By suddenly taking your slothful dog for several long walks a day, you could inadvertently cause him to suffer from overexertion, joint pain, or even a heart attack.

Since most dogs enjoy playing, it is a great tool for getting your English Cocker started in a more energetic routine. If your dog likes chasing his ball across the kitchen floor, start by throwing it across the backyard instead. (If your yard is not fenced, use an extendable leash to allow more freedom of movement.) As running becomes more of a regular part of your Cocker's day, extend the time period for his exercise sessions, but still watch for signs that your dog needs a break. Even the fittest animals benefit more from shorter, more frequent play periods than just one longer one.

As your dog begins to lose the extra weight, he will be better able to keep up with you on long walks, hikes, or even runs, but you must be patient. Expecting your portly pooch to literally run before he can walk will likely result in torn ligaments, serious pain, and costly surgeries. By taking things one solid step at a time, you will be introducing your dog (and possibly yourself as well) to a fit new lifestyle that you can enjoy together.

Don't forget to keep plenty of fresh drinking water available, especially when you venture away from home. Whether you are running around the block together or visiting the beach for a competitive game of Frisbee, you will need to replenish the fluids

you both lose while playing so hard.

Finally, you must be patient about the results from your dog's dieting and exercise efforts. The average human being usually only loses about a pound per week while trying to lose weight; excess weight will come off your English Cocker Spaniel even more slowly than this. However, by being consistent in your efforts to reduce your dog's weight, you *will* see results—and more importantly, improve his overall health—over time.

Mind Those Manners!

Begging comes in many different forms. Some dogs are more obvious in their approach: they fuss, whine, or outright bark to let you know that they want a bite of that tasty treat you're consuming. Others play it more subtly—they might just sit directly in front of you, not making a single sound, looking sad and hopeful. Although one method may be easier to deal with than the other, both should be discouraged. Most importantly, neither should ever be reinforced by giving in and feeding the dog the item in question.

If you think your English Cocker's begging habit is less of a problem because you hardly ever give in to his requests, you may be surprised to learn that he is probably more programmed to beg than you realize. Psychology 101 states that intermittent rewards actually reinforce behaviors better than consistent rewards.

If you want to stop your dog from begging, it can be done, but it will require a complete retraining process. In addition to abstaining from feeding your dog when he begs, you will also need to stop feeding him from the table—even if he isn't begging. All future treats must be placed directly into his dish, preferably from the counter and not the table. You must also completely ignore your Cocker when he begs—and he will, at least initially.

If your dog's begging habit has been deeply ingrained, provide a form of distraction for him during your meal or snack times. Feed your English Cocker along with the rest of the family, and then provide him with a special chew toy. This may be enough to do the trick, but if not, you might need to actually remove him from the room until the rest of the family is done eating. You can certainly give him the option of staying in the future, and he may or may not make the connection that when he begs, he has to go elsewhere.

The Drool Factor

If there is one thing that truly surprises me about Cocker Spaniels, it is how much they can drool! Before becoming a Cocker Spaniel owner so many years ago, I mistakenly assumed that drooling was something only larger dogs did (think of the movie *Beethoven* and you get the idea). I learned quickly, however, after getting my first Cocker that bigger dogs do *not* have this market cornered.

The most important thing to know about canine drooling is that it is extremely common and also healthy. Although it can be unpleasant to watch, drooling is an involuntary action, so no amount of training will help stop it from happening. If your dog's drooling is making your mealtimes less enjoyable for you or other family members, consider moving your dog to another room at these times. (If you feel guilty about exiling your beloved pet, make this a time for a special treat so that you are sure he does not see his removal as a punishment.)

Generally, a dog either drools or doesn't drool. If your English Cocker suddenly develops a drooling problem, mention it to your veterinarian. In extreme cases, this can indicate a medical problem. Also for this reason, let your vet know if your Cocker's drooling appears to increase in either frequency or amount.

Common Diseases and Injuries Related to Obesity

- Arthritis
- Cruciate ligament injury
- Diabetes
- Gastrointestinal problems
- Heart disease
- Kidney disease
- Luxating patella
- Musculoskeletal diseases
- Respiratory problems

If your dog is overweight, adjust his diet to include less calories and fat, and talk to your vet about stepping up his exercise regimen.

5

GROOMING
Your English Cocker Spaniel

An English Cocker Spaniel in full coat is a striking image, but one that can also be quite intimidating to a new owner. Rest assured that the long hair and luxuriant furnishings of a show Cocker are optional. Many owners find that keeping their dogs in a shorter pet clip is considerably more manageable, but even this will require at least weekly grooming. Most importantly, if you do decide that you want to keep your dog in a longer coat, be sure you have the time necessary to keep up with this more involved look. Even if you send your dog out for advanced grooming, you will still need to brush him daily.

Above and beyond the importance of keeping your dog clean and free of mats and tangles, regular grooming is an ideal opportunity for you to spend precious one-on-one time with your dog. As your Cocker learns to trust you to perform the various tasks involved, he will likely look forward to grooming sessions more and more. You will also be deepening the unique bond between you, making the entire grooming process seem like less of a job and more like a peaceful respite the two of you share.

START THEM OUT YOUNG!

The first step in establishing good grooming habits is showing your puppy that grooming can truly feel good. Begin brushing your dog with just your fingers alone, massaging his body as you gently work your fingertips through each section of fur. Don't forget the ears and paws, and be sure to praise your dog when you are finished.

It is never too early to start the process. By the time you bring your English Cocker Spaniel home, he will likely have already had his first bath and at least one haircut. To keep him looking great and to help him behave well during future grooming sessions, you must pick up where the breeder left off. Your dog may resist this process a bit at first, but bear in mind that you are setting important precedents. Your consistent efforts will pay off, but your early expectations must be reasonable. Getting your dog to simply tolerate a daily five-minute brushing session is a practical initial goal.

Keeping the sessions short is especially important during the introductory phase. It is the frequent repetition, not prolonged exposure to the tasks, which helps create a habit. As your dog begins to accept a brief brushing period, gradually lengthen the duration of each session until you are able to finish the job in one sitting. Always end the session on a positive note. Eventually, you might find that your dog, like many Cockers, looks forward to his daily brushing time. When you start early and maintain a regular brushing schedule, you avoid the nasty knots and snarls that make a dog fear being groomed.

Try to make grooming a special time for you and your dog to spend together. Your positive attitude will likely be contagious. Likewise, if you approach grooming as a chore to be dreaded, your dog will likely dread it, also.

GROOMING AS A HEALTH CHECK

Grooming also serves another very important purpose—helping to maintain your English Cocker Spaniel's health. Not only does regular grooming help prevent such problems as eye, ear, and even urinary infections, but it also provides you with the opportunity to examine your dog on a regular basis for anything unusual that might signal a health problem. Even after your dog acclimates to the brush, always begin each brushing session by using your bare

Begin grooming your English Cocker regularly from a young age to get him used to the process.

hands so that you can observe any changes in his coat or skin.

Look for anything that seems out of the ordinary. Your Cocker shouldn't have any unexplained cuts or sores, rashes or bumps, or fleas or ticks. Any abnormal growths are also a cause for concern. Although most turn out to be benign (harmless), even a malignant (cancerous) tumor can often be successfully removed when found early. Early detection is crucial in fighting virtually any canine disease or health problem.

Skin Care

Since English Cocker Spaniels have such long, beautiful fur, it is sometimes easy to overlook the importance of good skin care for these dogs. A particularly dry coat or skin may be a sign of illness, but there are other possible causes, as well. For example, bathing too frequently or using harsh shampoos can often cause itchy, dry skin. Insufficient rinsing can also lead to these problems.

When humans are stricken with allergies, we tend to suffer such symptoms as watery eyes, a runny nose, and sneezing. Dogs, on the other hand, react by itching. As dogs age, they become more susceptible to both skin and eye allergies. Interestingly, allergens can develop in areas that never previously posed a problem for your dog, so it can be extremely difficult to isolate the specific cause. Although blood tests are fairly inexpensive to perform, they tend not to be very reliable. If your dog appears to be suffering from an allergy, talk to your vet about performing an intradermal skin test. In this procedure (which is quite similar to the human version of the test), small amounts of allergens are injected beneath your dog's skin in hopes of identifying the precise cause of his allergic reaction.

Although it is crucial for you to identify the root of the problem, your dog only knows one thing: his skin feels irritated. Irritated skin leads to scratching, and uncontrolled scratching leads to infection. The most common canine allergen is fleas, but dogs can also suffer from inhaled allergens (pollen, for example) and food allergies. Although less common, dogs can even suffer from various forms of contact dermatitis.

Checking for Fleas

The best way to check your English Cocker Spaniel for fleas is by combing your dog and then shaking off any matter left on the comb onto a moistened piece of white paper or tissue. If a red stain appears as this matter begins to dissolve into the paper, your dog likely has fleas. (The red color is caused by ingested blood in the fleas' feces.)

BRUSHING AND COMBING

The most important thing you need to know about brushing your English Cocker Spaniel is that it should always be done before you bathe him. Getting a mat, even a bad one, out of dry hair is still remarkably easier than trying to remove it from wet fur, which is often virtually impossible. Knots also tend to retain soap, another reason to remove them before bathing. Brushing helps remove dirt and dead skin from your Cocker's fur, so keeping up with this task means that bathing will be necessary less frequently. Some owners find that a detangling spray is extremely helpful in removing knots, but be sure to follow the product's directions when using this grooming aid or you might find yourself intensifying the snarl by overwetting it.

In addition to having a dog riddled with knots, if you don't brush your Cocker regularly, he will be licking dirt and debris out of his fur whenever he self-grooms. Although this might seem harmless, you would likely be quite surprised by what can find its way into your dog's coat. My mother has always called her American Cocker Spaniel her "little dry mop" for this reason, as her Cocker's fur seems to rival the vacuum in how much it can pick up around the house. What owners cannot see, though, is usually even more dangerous—chemicals such as furniture polish, floor cleaners, and even lawn and garden treatments can end up on your pet's coat. No one knows the long-term effects that ingesting these substances might have on a canine pet.

Brushing Supplies

Many different types of brushes and combs are available, each offering distinctive advantages. Although you certainly won't need all of them, you will find that having more than just one kind is helpful. When you first bring your puppy home, his coat will be relatively short. For this reason, start with a soft-bristle brush that won't scratch your pup's delicate skin. As your Cocker's coat begins to grow, you will need something a bit more substantial to get the job done. A slicker brush serves this purpose very well, but you will still need to use care not to damage your pet's skin, as the wire bristles on this instrument can be abrasive when applied too roughly. A pin brush complete with plastic-tipped bristles is very easy on the skin, but it won't work as well as the slicker brush if your dog is prone to matting.

Your English Cocker's coat requires regular brushing and combing to keep it clean and free of mats.

How to Brush Your Cocker

Begin by brushing your dog's head and ears, then move on to his back, legs, chest, and belly. To remove as much dead hair as possible, first brush against the hair growth, and then brush with it. Although you don't want to hurt the skin, you do want to reach it. Cockers are considered average shedders, so daily brushings are certainly not too frequent, but in most situations brushing your dog once every three days should suffice. Remember, the more often you brush your dog, the less hair you will see on your clothes, carpet, and furniture. If he tends to get wet frequently, you may need to brush him more often.

Once you have thoroughly brushed your dog, it is time for combing. For the English Cocker Spaniel, the type of comb that works best is double-sided with wide teeth at one end and fine teeth at the other. The wide teeth are excellent for getting through the thicker parts of your dog's coat, whereas the fine teeth are better suited for the more delicate hair on the ears.

With their long ears and lower body furnishings, Cockers seem to get most of their mats on their ears and on the underside of their legs. If your dog has a really stubborn tangle that you cannot seem to get through with a brush or comb, a mat splitter may help destroy it. This sickle-shaped tool, available at most pet supply stores, literally shreds the mat for easy removal. Some people prefer placing a comb between the mat and the dog's skin and then cutting only the fur above the comb. While this may be equally effective, it may be more dangerous if your dog is a wiggler. If the mat is severe, and you are worried that you might accidentally hurt your dog by trying either of these methods, the best thing to do is bring your Cocker to a professional groomer.

You may also want to invest in a shedding blade. This curved metal tool that resembles a saw blade may be used with one hand (in its conventional looped position) or it may be used with its handles separated for two-hand use (with the blade straight). Many people find a shedding blade helpful for eliminating any loose hair left on your dog after brushing. It is also rather useful in removing excess water from your dog after a bath.

CLIPPING

Unlike some dog breeds that never require a single haircut, the English Cocker Spaniel needs his coat trimmed regularly. How often you wish to clip your dog's fur is up to you, but the longer you wait between haircuts, the longer and more tangle-prone your Cocker's fur will become. Of course, regular brushing will help prevent matting, but the longer the coat, the more involved brushing will be. If you plan to utilize your English Cocker Spaniel's field abilities, hand stripping is preferable to clipping to maintain the waterproof quality of his outer coat. Show Cockers, though, are usually groomed with clippers.

Grooming as Bonding Time

Not only is grooming time important for keeping your dog clean and comfortable, it is also an excellent opportunity for introducing your dog to the wonders of touch. Begin each session by gently massaging your dog with just your fingers, and never hesitate to stop a particular task long enough to give or receive a quick kiss. As you build his trust, you will find that both you and your Cocker look forward to the special time the grooming process provides. Few things are as satisfying as grooming an English Cocker Spaniel who is in complete accord with your efforts, especially when this same dog struggled adamantly against the process just a few weeks or months prior.

How to Clip Your Cocker

Clipping an English Cocker Spaniel is not an impossible job for an owner, but it does require some training and experience to do it well. If you have never handled a pair of electric dog clippers, you need to know a few things before deciding to groom your Cocker yourself. First and most importantly, you should always brush and bathe your dog before clipping. Dirt and debris from his coat can easily find their way into your shears; this can dull the blades, placing your dog at risk of unnecessary injury and shortening the life of the clippers.

The best way to learn how to groom an English Cocker Spaniel is by watching a knowledgeable person do the job. Ask your breeder if you may sit in on a grooming session or two so that you can observe this task first-hand. Perhaps you can even bring along your new puppy, so you can practice some of the techniques yourself in your breeder's presence. Although your veterinarian is often your best resource when it comes to your dog's health and overall care, remember that your breeder has the most experience in dealing with English Cocker Spaniels specifically. Never underestimate the value of this experience.

Instructional grooming videos may also be helpful (and are often included with grooming tools upon purchase), but nothing compares to the value of personal experience. The dogs featured in these videos are also on their best behavior—a whole different scenario from the wriggling Cocker pup you will likely encounter the first time your dog needs a clipping. As with all other parts of the grooming process, though, know that practice will help both you and your dog perform better over time.

Do I Need a Grooming Table?

Although it is important to teach your dog to stand for grooming, a grooming table is not a necessity for every English Cocker Spaniel owner. If you plan to show your dog, however, this item will likely come in quite handy. As many owners have learned, it is also a great back saver. Providing your dog with a sturdy, non-slip surface on which to stand, a grooming table also offers the added security of a safety harness.

Just like brushing, clipping is a task you want to begin early so that it becomes a normal part of your dog's routine. You may decide that keeping your Cocker in a shorter pet clip is the best option until you become more adept at clipping and your dog becomes more comfortable with the grooming process; or you both may take to it like a bird-dog to water.

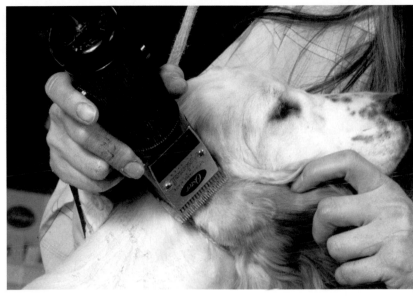

Ask your breeder or a professional groomer for help and advice before attempting to clip your English Cocker yourself.

BATHING THE BEAUTY

Once your English Cocker Spaniel has been thoroughly brushed and combed, it's time to start the bath. When your Cocker is a puppy, the kitchen sink may suffice as the basin for this task, but as he grows, the bathtub will become a more practical option. (It is also a completely acceptable place to bathe your puppy from the very beginning if you like.)

Supplies

In addition to several large, absorbent bath towels, you will need your Cocker's shampoo and conditioner, a cup for rinsing (if your shower does not have a movable spray nozzle), a washcloth, cotton balls, and mineral oil. A waterproof collar and leash may also be helpful. Make sure you gather all the necessary bathing supplies before you begin. Once your dog is in the water, you will not be able to run to grab that one item you forgot, so be sure not to miss anything.

Choosing a Shampoo

Since shampoos generally strip hair of its natural oils, select a product that will moisturize your dog's coat and skin. Although

Before his bath, provide your dog with a quick chance to relieve himself, since he won't have the opportunity again for a little while. This is particularly important if you are bathing your dog on a cool or windy day or in a particularly cold climate. Also with temperature in mind, check the thermostat before heading out the door to make sure the room is warm enough for when your dog gets out of his bath.

some people insist that frequent bathing alone will cause a Cocker's skin and fur to dry out, two factors make a huge difference in the veracity of this statement: a good-quality shampoo made especially for a canine coat and adequate rinsing. If these two issues are properly addressed, you should be able to bathe your English Cocker Spaniel as often as you like (within reason, of course) without drying either his coat or his skin. A bath every three to four weeks is a sensible interval, although some dogs can go much longer between baths without a problem. (A dog used in the field, for example, only needs a bath when his coat gets soiled.)

The selection of dog shampoos that greet you at the pet supply store might intimidate you just a bit. In addition to the good old-fashioned flea and tick shampoo that's been available for decades, now there are also tear-free, detangling, hypoallergenic, oatmeal, color-enhancing, medicated, anti-dandruff, and even aromatic varieties. Just like young human children, puppies require extra mild shampoos, and a wide array of products are made just for them, as well.

You might assume that allowing your dog to use your own shampoo, especially an expensive salon brand, is a nice way to spoil your beloved Cocker. Although your heart may be in the right place, you will actually be doing your pet a great disservice by not purchasing a canine product. Whereas human hair is rather acidic (5.6 on the pH scale), a dog's skin has an alkaline pH (6.7 to 7.8). A dog's skin is also considerably thinner than ours, leaving it particularly vulnerable to irritation from products designed with a human's body chemistry in mind.

If you want to spoil your dog with special bathing indulgences, you still have many options. Just browse through that vast assortment of shampoos at the pet supply store. You will likely find at least one brand even more expensive than the products in your own shower caddy. One very famous salon now offers a line of high-end pet grooming products. Perhaps your Cocker would enjoy the calming scent of chamomile or the tick-repelling benefits of Australian tea tree oil for his next bath?

How to Bathe Your Cocker

First, to protect your Cocker against slipping and falling, have your dog stand on a safety mat inside the tub. Next, place a dry cotton ball in each of your dog's ears, then fully saturate the dog's coat with lukewarm water. (Always remember to check the water temperature before wetting your dog.) Getting the water to reach your dog's skin requires a fair amount of water pressure, so if you don't already have a shower massager, consider investing in one. While your Cocker is still a puppy, a sink sprayer should serve this purpose fine, but bear in mind that bathing your adult English Cocker Spaniel in the kitchen sink will unlikely be an option. Whether using the tub or sink, it is not necessary to submerge your dog in water at the beginning of the bath. If you do fill the basin with water, though, be sure to let this water drain completely before rinsing your dog.

Never apply shampoo until your dog is thoroughly wet, as this will only dry out his coat. Next, dispense a small amount of shampoo into your hands, rubbing them together to work up a good lather before applying the product to your dog. Starting at the head, work your way downward and toward the tail, adding more shampoo as needed. Avoid soaping your dog's eyes and ears. Leave the shampoo on for the recommended time, as some medicated and conditioning shampoos require that the product remain on the animal for several minutes.

Reaction to Shampoo

If your dog's skin shows any negative reaction to the shampoo you choose, like redness, rash, or severe itching, you may need to switch to a medicated or hypoallergenic product. Consult your veterinarian before applying anything else, though, as your dog's skin may need a chance to heal first. By adding another product into the mix too early, you could make it more difficult to isolate and diagnose the problem.

Rinse, Repeat

The next step—rinsing—is without a doubt the most important part of the shampooing process. When you are ready to rinse, check the water to make sure it is still only lukewarm, and thoroughly rinse all the shampoo out of your dog's coat. When you are absolutely certain you have rinsed out every bit of shampoo, rinse your dog well at least one more time.

Conditioners

Some people may balk at the idea of using conditioner on a dog, but the truth of the matter is that English Cocker Spaniel hair isn't always naturally silky; sometimes it needs a little help. A high-quality conditioner can be just as important as your dog's shampoo. In addition to providing your dog's skin with essential fatty acids to help reduce dryness, a good conditioner aids in the grooming process by reducing static electricity. It may even help prevent mats from forming.

Like waterless shampoos, conditioners are also available in rinse-free varieties. One of these may be sufficient for a dog with

Bathe your English Cocker with a quality shampoo made specifically for dogs to keep his coat and skin in top condition.

less intense conditioning needs. Or if your English Cocker Spaniel is one of the lucky ones already blessed with a soft, manageable coat, consider using a homemade vinegar and water rinse instead. Made by stirring a tablespoon of white vinegar into a pint of warm water, this solution will help remove excess soap and prevent dandruff from forming. Simply rub the solution into your dog's coat, then rinse well with plain water.

After applying the conditioner or rinse, dampen your washcloth and gently wash your dog's face. Next, remove the cotton balls from your Cocker's ears and gently wipe the insides with another pair of cotton balls moistened with mineral oil. This helps to maintain lubrication in the ear, which reduces the build-up of wax and other debris.

Blow-drying

There are several good reasons for blow-drying your English Cocker Spaniel. On a nice day, allowing your dog to air-dry is a perfectly acceptable option, providing that you make a point of brushing him periodically as his coat dries. On a colder day, however, it is important that you help your dog's hair follicles close with a moderate amount of heat. A wet dog is also especially vulnerable to dirt. This is another reason you want to provide a potty break before the bath—a wet dog is inexplicably drawn to rolling around in the grass and dirt as soon as he goes outdoors.

If your Cocker has a full coat, you will probably want to brush him throughout the blow-drying process. This will help to prevent post-bath tangles from forming and will also help to straighten the coat. While a slight wave is permissible in conformation, a Cocker with a curly or cottony coat will be harshly penalized. You may also find that the feet tend to feather more easily with the use of an electric dryer.

Your Cocker puppy may initially be frightened by the foreboding sound of the blow dryer. Rest assured that this is a very normal reaction that should pass with consistent exposure. Never try to scare your dog with any noisy object, though, as this will only reinforce a fear of loud sounds. To help avoid compounding the problem with a nasty burn, always keep your hand between the dryer and your dog, and keep the machine on a low to medium setting.

Blow the air in the direction of hair growth, and continue to brush your dog as his hair dries. More hair will shed as he dries, so finish with another brushing session when blow-drying is complete. This is also an ideal time to use the shedding blade.

EAR CARE

Bath time offers an excellent opportunity for cleaning your dog's ears, but this should only be one part of your dog's ear-cleaning routine. Since an English Cocker Spaniel's ears are particularly prone to *otitis externa* (ear infection), frequent cleaning is recommended.

Unlike humans, dogs have an L-shaped ear canal. Breeds with upright ears (such as the Boxer and German Shepherd) tend to get better airflow into this area, therefore reducing the amount of moisture and bacteria inside the ear. Long, drooping ears weighted with long hair, in contrast, hang over the ear canal, creating a prolific environment for infection. Ideally, a Cocker's ears should be cleaned twice weekly, or more often if your dog has suffered repeated ear infections.

The first step in proper canine ear care is visual examination of each ear. A healthy ear should be pink (not red) inside and free of swelling or any kind of discharge. Next, sniff the ear—it shouldn't smell strong or at all foul. If you discover anything unusual while inspecting your Cocker's ears, refrain from cleaning and instead defer to your veterinarian for further examination and treatment. Other signs of ear infection include frequent head shaking, leaning the head to one side, pawing at the ear, and sensitivity to touch.

While it may be tempting to wash away any discharge you find in your Cocker's ears, resist doing so—swabbing this area will likely be your vet's most important step in diagnosing the problem. Also, cleaning an already infected ear can also further irritate an area that is already extremely tender and sore. If you suspect a problem with your Cocker's ears, it is vital that you bring him for veterinary care. Although you may be able to flush the ear at home, problems such as mites and infections cannot be cured by simple

Waterless Shampoo

Waterless shampoos are a great way to clean your English Cocker when a conventional bath is not feasible. Sold in most pet supply stores, these rinse-free products are especially helpful for bathing after a surgical procedure or helping your dog stay clean (and dry!) on those blustery days when a wet bath might not be ideal. Incidentally, your pantry cupboard probably already contains one of the best waterless dog shampoos around—cornstarch. A very versatile substance indeed, cornstarch can also serve as a styptic powder if you should accidentally cut a toenail too short during your Cocker's pedicure.

hygiene—they demand veterinary attention and medication.

Supplies

Ear-cleaning solutions and wipes are available at your local pet supply store. While extremely effective as antiseptics, many of these products contain isopropyl alcohol and hydrogen peroxide. These ingredients can be too harsh for dogs already suffering from an ear problem or for those with sensitive skin. Your veterinarian can likely offer you a milder solution, or you can make your own from equal parts of vinegar and water.

How to Clean Your Cocker's Ears

To apply the cleaner, squirt a liberal amount of the product directly into your dog's ear and then rub the ear in a downward motion for approximately 30 seconds. Most dogs shake their heads immediately following this step, which actually helps loosen dirt imbedded within the ear. Next use cotton balls (never cotton swabs) to gently wipe the inside of the ear. Be sure not to go beyond the 90-degree turn within the ear that leads to your dog's inner ear.

At first, the cotton ball will be stained a dark color—this means you are effectively removing the dirt. As you continue, the color will lighten as less and less dirt appears. This is how you determine when the ear has been sufficiently cleaned. Remember, a small amount of wax is necessary to properly coat your Cocker's ear canal, so don't expect the cotton to come out completely white. It is also especially important to be gentle when cleaning your dog's ears, since an overly vigorous cleaning can leave even a healthy ear irritated and sore.

While you want to make sure you are using enough cleaner, be careful not to overdo it. A couple of squirts in each ear should be enough. Any more than this can leave the inside of your dog's ear too wet, and infections flourish in moist environments. For this same reason,

Your English Cocker's long ears are particularly prone to infection and require frequent cleaning.

Ear Advice for the Summer

In warm weather, make sure that the hair on the inside of the ear is kept trimmed short. This will allow air to circulate and help to keep the ear healthy. Also, when your dog has been out for a run during the summer months, always check that he doesn't have any grass awns (seeds with long, sharp, spiky cases) lodged in his ears or feet. These can work their way up inside the ear or foot by friction and can cause great pain.

(Courtesy of The Cocker Spaniel Club)

make an effort to keep your dog's ears dry at other times, as well. Friends of mine have a Cocker Spaniel who loves to swim in their pool whenever he gets the chance. Unfortunately, he suffers from frequent ear infections from having water in his ears so frequently.

You may notice that your English Cocker Spaniel has hair inside his ears. You may shave or clip this hair to allow for better airflow into the ear, but never pull it out. Pulling can leave tiny wounds that are especially vulnerable to bacteria and subsequent infection. Pulling can also be quite painful for your dog. If you think the hair needs to be extracted, consult your veterinarian.

EYE CARE

Many English Cocker Spaniels produce a fair amount of eye discharge. If left on the face for an extended time, these eye secretions can harden and be rather difficult to remove from the dog's fur. Wiping your dog's eyes daily with a damp cloth should prevent this crusty matter from forming. If the hair around your dog's eyes is a light color, you may also notice some tear staining from eye discharge. Using distilled water on your cleaning cloth can help keep these stains to a minimum.

Eye secretions should always be clear and watery, never colored or mucous-like. Other problem signs include redness, itching, or squinting. If you notice any of these symptoms, consult your veterinarian. While the problem may be as simple as conjunctivitis (pink eye), the symptoms may be due to a more serious ocular or neurological problem. Any changes in pupil size and reactivity are a particular cause for concern and demand immediate veterinary attention.

Keeping Your Puppy's Ears Clean

Some dogs, especially younger dogs, may produce excess wax while the ear canal is still developing. You can clean this extra wax by administering ear drops obtained from pet shops, chemists, or vets.

(Courtesy of The Cocker Spaniel Club)

NAIL CARE

Some grooming tasks are definitely more intimidating than others. For many dog owners, nail trimming undoubtedly falls into the daunting category. Unlike human nails, canine toenails vary in color from dog to dog (even within the same breed). Recognizing the nerve center, commonly called the "quick" or "nail bed", can be especially challenging in dogs whose fur and nails match extremely closely. Cut the nail too short, and you can cut the quick and cause profuse pain and bleeding; leave the nail untrimmed altogether, and you risk even worse problems.

The importance of keeping your English Cocker Spaniel's nails trimmed cannot be emphasized enough. Overgrown nails can catch on clothing, carpeting, and even the dog's own fur. (Dewclaws, the superfluous claws situated high on most dogs' feet, are particularly prone to this. Your breeder may remove your Cocker's dewclaws before you bring your puppy home, but if not, be constantly vigilant in keeping them properly trimmed.) Toenails that catch can easily be pulled completely out of your dog's foot—an event as painful as it sounds and one that can lead to the dislocation of a toe. Long nails can also curl under and pierce the dog's pads like an agonizing ingrown toenail.

To start nail trimming off on the right foot, so to speak, begin handling your dog's feet and toes regularly when he is still a puppy. If your dog seems sensitive to this, it is even more important that you make this effort. Lightly massage his paws daily to build trust and help him perceive having his feet touched as just an ordinary part of his routine.

Be careful not to cut the quick (nail bed) when trimming your English Cocker's nails.

Supplies

A few different models of nail clippers are available at most pet supply stores. With guillotine style clippers, you place your dog's nail into a hole in the unit before squeezing the handles to cut the nail. Pliers style clippers that cut from side to side are particularly handy in getting through harder nails. Scissors style clippers, which closely resemble a pair of human manicure scissors, have a special blade made for cutting canine toenails. None of the three styles does a better job than the others, but many guillotine and pliers clippers feature a built-in stopper that helps prevent users from cutting too much of the nail—an important bonus for many nervous owners.

How to Trim Your Cocker's Nails

To trim your Cocker's toenails with a conventional pair of clippers, first gently spread his toes. Inspect the areas between them, carefully cleaning away any debris with a damp cloth or moist cotton ball. Next, holding your dog's foot firmly, push gently on the pad to extend the nail. Once you have identified the quick—when visible, it will be pink—snip off only the hook-like end of the nail on a 45-degree angle, without getting too close to the quick. Remember, you can always cut more if necessary, but if you cut too much, you arrive at a regretful point of no return.

Immediately after a trim, your dog's nails will likely feel especially sharp. This can be easily remedied by using a canine-grade nail file to smooth the edges. You may also combine the two tasks by using a nail grinder instead of a conventional pair of clippers. This electric- or battery-powered rotary tool trims the toenail by grinding it down. One obvious advantage to a nail grinder is that it automatically cauterizes any wounds when used at higher speeds.

Regardless of the tool you select, take your time, and allow your Cocker some time to adjust to the procedure as well. Offer short breaks based on your dog's tolerance—in the very beginning, you might have to spread the task over a day or more.

Never underestimate the importance of both patience and rewards. These two keys to preventing your dog from feeling overwhelmed will help him accept nail trimming as an inevitable part of his routine, even if he doesn't particularly enjoy having it done. Edible rewards can be extremely effective for nurturing tolerance, but bear in mind that treats should never replace frequent verbal praise—a powerful reward in itself.

"Quick" Fact

Interestingly, the quick recedes a bit with each trimming so that clipping a small amount regularly actually helps prevent you from accidentally injuring your dog during future trims.

DENTAL CARE

One of the most overlooked causes for many canine health problems is poor dental health. Although the most obvious effect of neglecting your dog's teeth and gums is periodontal disease, bear in mind that your English Cocker Spaniel swallows bacteria from the plaque and tartar accumulating in his mouth. These harmful microorganisms are then transported throughout your dog's body, leaving it vulnerable to countless medical problems, including heart and kidney disease. Older dogs are especially susceptible to this threat, but poor oral hygiene increases the risk of disease in dogs of any age.

Once formed on your dog's teeth, calculus (the medical term for tartar) is nearly impossible to remove without professional help from a veterinarian. In addition to being costly, a cleaning of this kind also requires that your dog be anesthetized—something that should only be done when absolutely necessary. Professional teeth cleaning is a double-edged sword: Your dog's teeth need to be clean in order for him to be healthy, but when left to accumulate, plaque and tartar can ultimately cause a problem making the required anesthesia a greater risk to your pet. The best solution is to avoid this dilemma entirely and brush your dog's teeth yourself on a regular basis.

Taking care of your dog's teeth at home reduces the likelihood of periodontal disease and other dental problems that require veterinary attention.

Like trimming your Cocker's nails, brushing his teeth will likely demand a certain amount of patience on your behalf. Also like nail trimming, making dental care a part of your dog's regular routine early on will help foster his tolerance for it. Since this task should be performed more often than many others, it is especially important that you start early.

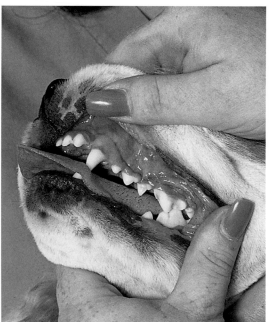

Supplies

A canine toothbrush kit can be purchased from most pet supply retailers. This usually includes a long, angled brush with a large head at one end and a smaller one at the other, a bristled finger brush, and a tube of canine toothpaste. You can also purchase these items individually, as well as specially flavored toothpastes in enticing varieties such as beef, poultry, and seafood. Don't use toothpaste intended for humans—although your toothpaste may cleanse your dog's teeth, it is not intended for dogs and can even make them sick.

You don't even have to invest in a

toothbrush kit if you don't want to—a small piece of wet cotton gauze can serve as an excellent toothbrush.

How to Brush Your Cocker's Teeth

Like canine nail trimming, tooth brushing can be an acquired taste for your Cocker. If he appears to be resisting all aspects of the task, start by simply getting him used to the feel of your fingers inside his mouth, then gradually move on to using gauze or a finger brush. Use the finger brush or gauze daily to help establish the tooth brushing habit. Once you have some success with this, add a small amount of toothpaste. (You can also introduce him to the toothpaste by simply offering a small amount on your finger— unlike human toothpaste, canine toothpaste won't hurt your dog if it is swallowed.)

Battling Bad Breath

To help neutralize and prevent doggy breath, add a small amount of fresh rosemary or finely chopped parsley to your English Cocker Spaniel's food. But remember, plaque and tartar are most often the culprits behind foul-smelling breath, so keep brushing those teeth!

Most importantly, remain both patient and consistent. If your English Cocker tolerates the finger brush but balks when you introduce a longer, more conventional toothbrush, there is actually no need to make the transition as long as you are getting your dog's teeth clean.

Using a circular motion, gently wipe your dog's teeth with the gauze or toothbrush, paying particular attention to the area where the teeth meet the gums—the spot where tartar tends to accumulate the most. When you are finished brushing, rinse his teeth with either a damp cloth or a squeeze bottle. Although rinsing is not technically necessary, it will help leave your Cocker's mouth feeling cleaner and more refreshed.

Ideally, you should brush your English Cocker Spaniel's teeth every day. If you find this schedule too stringent, just try to brush as often as you can. Offering hard treats, such as dog biscuits and raw carrots, between brushings can help fight the buildup of plaque and tartar, as can the use of safe chew toys like Nylabones. Offering your dog a dry-food diet will also assist in this area. None of these things, however, can replace the fundamental task of brushing. If you feed wet or homecooked food, daily brushing is a near necessity.

SELECTING A PROFESSIONAL GROOMER

Grooming is a task that, to some degree, all dog owners must perform. Individual tasks such as brushing your English Cocker

If You Cut the Quick

If you inadvertently cut below your dog's quick, the most important thing is to remain calm. Promptly apply a styptic powder or pencil to the cut to speed clotting. Although cornstarch can serve as an impromptu styptic powder, you can also use a wet tea bag or a soft bar of soap. Simply apply the tea bag firmly to the affected area, or push your dog's nail into the bar until the bleeding subsides.

If you find yourself repeatedly nicking your dog during nail trims, you may want to consider entrusting the responsibility to someone with more experience. Either your veterinarian or a professional groomer can assume this task for you. English Cocker Spaniels can be amazingly forgiving creatures, but no dog should be expected to withstand continual cuts. Repeated accidents may also likely trigger a deeply ingrained fear of nail trimming.

Spaniel's coat, for instance, must be done regularly at home in order for your dog to remain happy and healthy. Certain other tasks, however, may be delegated to someone else if necessary.

For some Cocker owners, the biggest challenge is time. Perhaps you can keep up with the necessary tasks of brushing and nail trimming, but you find yourself constantly postponing your dog's bath to when things calm down a bit—an elusive time that unfortunately never materializes. For others, just the prospect of trying to duplicate the stylish Cocker clip seems like a more challenging mission than splitting an atom. Luckily, professional dog groomers can fill these important niches.

Deciding to send your dog to a groomer is only the first step. Next, you must find a groomer who will fulfill your grooming needs while treating your dog with the same amount of care and respect as you do. It is of the utmost importance that you trust not only this person's abilities, but also her genuine fondness for animals. More than anything else, listen to your instincts, but you can also use the following criteria to narrow your selection.

Choosing a groomer is a lot like selecting a daycare provider. You will, after all, be leaving your English Cocker Spaniel in this person's charge for the better part of a day, each time he needs to be groomed. Ask many questions and carefully inspect the facilities before making your decision.

Where to Find a Groomer

Although you can easily find a dog groomer by simply thumbing through your local phonebook, a better place to start is with your breeder, veterinarian, or a friend who also owns an

English Cocker Spaniel. Recommendations from these trusted individuals are invaluable, and prevent you from having to start your search based on such superficial information as which business has the best ad. Another good resource for new dog owners seeking a groomer is the National Dog Groomers Association of America.

Bear in mind that no government agency regulates or licenses pet groomers. Although many groomers are registered or certified by their individual training schools or other organizations, it is still extremely important to interview a potential groomer and tour the facilities before leaving your Cocker there.

Initial questions may pertain to costs, hours of operation, and other general policies. If you think the business may be able to meet your needs, ask for references and follow up by contacting them. You should also contact the Better Business Bureau to find out if any complaints have been filed against the company.

If your dog is overdue for grooming, you mustn't expect to drop off a severely matted dog and pick up a perfectly coifed English Cocker Spaniel in full coat. Although you don't have to meet every one of your dog's grooming needs personally, visiting a professional groomer a few times a year cannot remedy months of neglect between appointments. A groomer can be an excellent partner in your dog's grooming needs, but even the most talented professionals cannot brush out months of neglect. Even if this were possible, it wouldn't be fair to your dog either.

A professional dog groomer can perform the grooming tasks that you are unable or hesitant to do yourself.

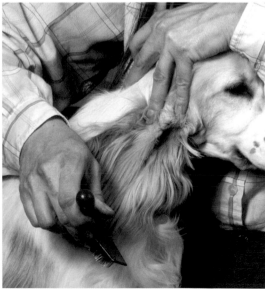

Even if you don't plan on depending on someone else for grooming, it may be a wise idea to utilize this kind of service at least occasionally. Helping your English Cocker Spaniel become more comfortable in the hands of others can only have a positive effect on his temperament. At the very least, it may be an excellent exercise in socialization that offers you a pleasant break in the process.

Chapter

6

TRAINING *and* BEHAVIOR

of Your English Cocker Spaniel

When I was a little girl, there was only one well-known dog trainer in the area of Maine where I grew up. His television ads explained succinctly how he could train your dog for you, and there was always a Doberman Pinscher in these commercials. The breed was chosen, I imagine, because it looked imposing, and this fit the image most people had at that time of a dog in need of formal training.

Today, dog owners realize that a more universal need for dog training exists. Although many of us still turn to professional instructors, we also prefer to be more involved than in the past. The dog training industry has evolved into a versatile medium in which we can take classes in group settings, read books or watch videos that detail the various methods of training, or use a combination of these resources to teach our dogs what they need to know—all while remaining an integral part of the process ourselves. Most of us have even discovered that we can bond deeply with our animals through this often-exciting undertaking.

Not all types of training are pleasant, of course. Housetraining immediately springs to mind when I think of the more intimidating of training tasks. Like other kinds of training, housetraining demands a solid commitment of both time and effort, but it also offers an opportunity to increase your dog-training knowledge and build your confidence for the many other types of lessons that lie ahead. Positive reinforcement for a job well done goes a long way with our canine friends. They seem to instinctively want to please us, and it is our responsibility to show them how to do just that.

WHAT KIND OF TRAINING DOES MY ENGLISH COCKER NEED?

You may feel overwhelmed by just the jargon alone: crate training, clicker training, basic obedience—somehow it doesn't sound so basic when you are looking at your brand-new puppy and worrying about whether you will be able to snag him that last highly coveted spot in puppy kindergarten. Some trainers even suggest placing your dog in a puppy playgroup as an additional means of early socialization.

Wait a minute, you might be thinking. Puppy kindergarten? Playgroups? Although this might sound a bit extreme to a new dog owner, it is actually very practical advice. There is no need to feel overwhelmed. By following a few simple instructions and taking things one step at a time, you should be able to place your pup on the road to excellent training in no time.

But He's a Housedog!

Many people feel that "housedogs" don't need formal obedience training, and this might indeed be the case, but bear in mind that dogs will learn no matter how formal their education. If no direction is provided, it's all a matter of what the dog decides is worth learning. Very much like children, dogs pay close attention to their surroundings and acclimate to them accordingly. Also like children, animals thrive in at least somewhat structured environments. Rules help keep everyone safe.

Positive training methods will yield the best results with your English Cocker Spaniel.

Even if you never plan to teach your English Cocker Spaniel any other formal commands, I urge you to consider just one—*come*. Learning to obey this one simple directive could literally save your dog's life. You may think of your house as secure as Fort Knox, and you might feel certain that your dog would never bolt even if given the opportunity, but the fact is that many smart, beloved dogs escape the safety of their homes every day. With the threats of motor vehicles, wild animals, and extreme weather conditions always lurking, it is always good to have one more safety precaution in place.

Training, as long as the tone is kept positive, is never a waste of time. Even if you never plan to involve your dog in obedience trials, if you enjoy teaching your dog commands just for fun, go

Canine Body Language at a Glance

Like most other breeds, English Cocker Spaniels seem to have a remarkable understanding of human emotion. For example, how many times has your dog seemed to know instantly when you were feeling sad and could use a special pick-me-up from your best canine pal? Perhaps this is due in part to a dog's intrinsic awareness of human body language. Unfortunately, some owners are far less perceptive about the emotions their dogs are experiencing. Dogs do offer us clues, though—we just have to look for them.

When it comes to certain displays of canine body language, some breeds are easier to read than others. It can be difficult to tell with a floppy eared dog like an English Cocker whether his ears are forward, flattened, or perked, but if you look closely, you will see that there *are* variations. It can also be tricky to determine how your dog is feeling based on just one part of his appearance alone. A dog with his ears lying flat against his head, for instance, might be feeling submissive or aggressive depending on his other body postures. Always consider all the aspects of your dog's outward appearance when trying to interpret his body language, and listen to your own intuition, as well, as this can often be very accurate.

	EARS	EYES	BODY	TAIL
Aggressive	Forward or flattened against head	Wide open, making direct contact	Standing tall, chest thrust forward, raised hackles (hairs on back)	Straight up, out, or wagging slowly and stiffly
Alert	Perked up	Open normally or wide	Very tall position—looking slightly dominant	Carried at 45-degree angle or higher, possible wagging
Curious	Perked up	Wide open	Wiggling, possibly standing tiptoed	Up and wagging
Fearful	Flattened against head	Averted or narrowed	Tense or trembling	Wagging droopily
Guarding	Perked up	Wide open	Tense, but standing very tall	Straight out from body
Playful	Perked up	Lively	Elbows lowered with bottom in the air (play bow), or a raised front paw	Wagging
Submissive	Flattened against head	Averted, narrowed, or half-closed	Contracted, as if to appear smaller, or rolled onto back	Tucked under or exaggerated wagging (seeming to wag the whole bottom)

ahead and do it. You may want to work with him in the privacy of your own home for a while before deciding whether more organized training activities are right for both of you. There is no "correct" choice, just the one that is right for you and your dog.

SELECTING A TRAINER

The concept of "sending" a dog to a trainer always struck me as an undermining practice. Sure, the dog may learn a variety of commands and might even be able to demonstrate them initially upon his return home, but will he respond to you as well as he did to the person who trained him? Certainly, a trainer has a valuable role in the process of teaching our dogs what we want them to do, but that role should focus more on teaching *us* how to train our dogs than on taking these fundamental steps for us.

A veterinarian or local animal shelter may be able to refer you to a reputable dog trainer.

With this objective in mind, the first guideline for finding an effective dog trainer is making sure the instructor views her clients as partners in the dog-training process. A responsible trainer should be willing to answer any questions or concerns that you have, but will also expect you to listen and do your part. It is also wise to have your dog meet this person before finalizing your arrangements, since a good rapport with your English Cocker Spaniel is ideal.

Where to Find a Trainer

Nowadays, trainers can be found virtually everywhere—through business cards posted at your local pet store, in your phone book's yellow pages, and even online. Selecting the right one, however, requires a bit more effort. With so many different training methods part of the mainstream, you should first start with the style of training that you desire (leash and collar, reward-based, clicker training, etc.). Second, ask for referrals from your veterinarian or local animal shelter, as these resources will lead you to the most reputable trainers in your area. You may also contact the Association of Pet Dog Trainers at (800) PET-DOGS or www.apdt. com for the name of a trainer near you. Knowledge of canine health and behavior, as well as experience with English Cocker Spaniels specifically, is definitely a plus.

Set Goals

Have clear goals for what you want your dog to learn, and be sure to communicate them to the trainer. Perhaps there is a particular problem behavior (such as nipping) that you want your dog to discontinue. While basic commands are all useful in their own right, teaching your dog to sit, stay, and come will do nothing to solve your nipping problem if you don't make the issue known to your trainer.

Finally, remember that training takes time and that you should always maintain a positive attitude. When your dog "gets it," praise him abundantly. When he doesn't, try to remain patient. Never use punishment as a way of teaching your English Cocker Spaniel anything, for all you will actually teach him by doing so is to fear you. Negative reactions such as yelling, hitting, jerking your dog's leash, or isolating him will only decrease his motivation— and damage your relationship.

Also, never underestimate the power of praise. While simply ignoring a failed attempt may seem like an inefficient act, it will in fact encourage results, since what any dog wants most is to please his loving owner. Ending on a positive note is also a smart idea. By doing so, both you and your dog will be more likely to return to the process at a later time with the best possible attitude toward training.

INVOLVING THE WHOLE FAMILY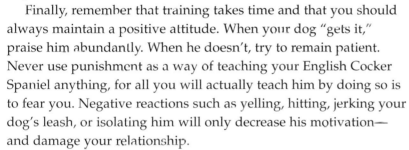

If you want your English Cocker Spaniel to be a true family dog, all family members will need to make an effort. A dog who is trained by only one person responds by depending on that person (and only that person) for all his needs. Chances are good that your dog will always see you as his leader, but it is important that he accepts others as loving caregivers as well.

Children in particular should play an important role in the training process. Being the pack-oriented animals that they are, maturing puppies can begin to view children within the household

Each member of your family should be involved in training your English Cocker.

as their contemporaries, and may even muster enough courage to challenge one of them for a higher-ranking position in the family. This is clearly not ideal, so placing your child in a position of authority from the start can head off this problem before it has a chance to rear its ugly head. This need not be difficult. Your preschooler may not be able to fully grasp the details of teaching your dog verbal commands, but she *can* assume a role as a loving superior by being placed in charge of feeding your English Cocker his meals each day or joining in praising your dog for a housetraining job well done.

Children who learn how to properly care for and respect animals will likely grow up to be responsible pet owners themselves. By empowering your child with a role in training your English Cocker Spaniel, you will not only be safeguarding them both from potential rivalry issues, but you will also be exposing your child to one of the most rewarding parts of life—the loving relationships that result from the humane treatment of animals.

CRATE TRAINING

I make no secret that at one time I was the furthest thing from a fan of the crate training process. I point this out now as a testament to the universal nature of this training method—if I could be convinced, anyone can. My purpose is not to sell you on using a crate, however, but rather to provide you with some of the information that I was lacking when I formed my own original opinions about crating so long ago. Whether you detest the idea of a crate even more than I once did or you consider it the one dog-training tool you could never be without, what matters most is that you go the route that's best for you and your English Cocker Spaniel. Like so many other resources, how you use it is even more important than if you choose to try it in the first place.

Is a Crate Right for Your English Cocker Spaniel?

First and perhaps most importantly, let's talk about what a crate *isn't*. The crate is not a place for punishment. If your dog has a housetraining accident, the crate can be a convenient spot to place him while you dispose of the mess, but the act of putting

Puppy Classes

Teaching your dog basic training and social skills cannot be started early enough. As soon as your puppy has completed his vaccination program, enrolling with a good puppy class will help you to build your relationship with your dog, understand how he learns, and help you to teach him some basic manners.

- Always visit a puppy class without your puppy before you book, and look for the following criteria:
- Exercises should be broken into small sessions suitable for puppies to learn.
- Puppies and people should look relaxed and happy.
- Punitive methods or equipment should not be in use. Choke chains, tight slip collars, and prong collars are not necessary.
- Noise should be kept to a minimum — shouting is unnecessary and lots of barking can indicate that the dogs are stressed.
- Instructors should be approachable. Do they appear friendly and caring of the best interests of owner and pup?
- How many puppies are there in the class? Bear in mind the size of the venue, as well as the number of assistants. Can the instructor keep an eye on everyone?
- Methods should suit the dog and handler in question. Food and toys are excellent motivators — not many dogs work for praise alone.
- Play between puppies should be carefully supervised and controlled and combined with gentle, effective training

(Courtesy of the Association of Pet Dog Trainers)

him inside should never include admonishment, and he should be released promptly once the soiled area has been cleaned. It makes sense that if you want your dog to consider his crate a refuge, you cannot use it as a prison.

Second, the crate is also not a place to keep your English Cocker Spaniel for hours on end. A dog should never be left in a crate for longer than he can reasonably hold his urine or feces. You should also always give your dog a chance to relieve himself before entering the crate and again after leaving it. Part of the reason why the crate is such a powerful housetraining tool is that dogs possess an innate preference not to soil the area in which they sleep. When a dog is confined in his crate for an unrealistic amount of time, he will be forced to overcome this natural aversion, defeating the whole purpose of using the crate as a housetraining tool. Also, the amount of time your dog spends resisting the need to eliminate can result in a serious infection.

Finally, the crate isn't for all dogs. You may think the crate-training concept sounds practical for your household, but a chance exists that your English Cocker Spaniel might simply not take to it. If your dog shows an irrational amount of fear toward crating, don't force the issue. This is not a problem that can be solved easily. The best solution is to avoid the issue entirely by providing your dog with another safe place to rest and sleep within your home, such as a gated room that has been puppy-proofed, when you cannot supervise him.

Likewise, if you aren't comfortable with crate training, don't do it. No rule states that proper dog care must involve the use of a crate. The choices we all make relating to pet care are often very subjective issues. Just ask several different people whether their dogs are allowed on the furniture, and you will likely get a mixture of answers. If you are deciding whether you should crate your English Cocker Spaniel or if he should sleep on your bed, the only correct answers address what's right for each individual dog and his owner.

Getting Started

While a crate must be of adequate size for your English Cocker Spaniel (large enough for him to comfortably stand up, lie down, and turn around inside), this is one item for which bigger isn't better. If you plan to use the crate as a housetraining aid, you will find it to be completely useless if it is too large. A dog who isn't trained won't hesitate to use one end of an overly spacious crate for a bathroom.

The placement of your dog's crate is another important concern. If he prefers having regular time to himself, situate the crate in an area away from the normal commotion of your home, like an office or a den. Or if he can't seem to get enough of being surrounded by his busy family, try to carve out a spot closer to a high-traffic area, such as your kitchen.

Although many dogs develop an immediate interest in the crate, you mustn't expect yours to necessarily jump right in with all four feet, so to speak. Your dog may be absolutely fascinated with this new hideaway—until, that is, you try to close the door. Even if his initial reaction to the crate is generally positive, the best way to introduce this new item is slowly.

Praise your dog whenever he makes any progress with his

What's in a Name?

Some authorities propose that the best names for dogs are those consisting of two syllables. The thought process behind this is that a name should be short, but a dog should never confuse his name with one of his commands, which are usually a single syllable. Similarly, many trainers also stress the importance of all family members calling their dog by the same name, as opposed to individual nicknames. The reason behind this is an animal's need for consistency.

Just as being called by different names can confuse a dog, being given inconsistent commands can also cause significant regression for a dog in the middle of training. The more that other people help to reinforce the commands you have taught your dog, the better. In fact, even though space is often limited, some trainers encourage participants to bring along as many family members to class as possible.

crate—whether this means entering for the first time, tolerating a closed door for just a couple of minutes, or running to his crate when you start leaving him in it regularly. Although the treat ball is a great idea, you need not offer a food reward; any special toy that you only offer while he is inside the crate may work.

If you do use a treat ball, consider tossing in a few pieces of your pup's kibble instead of an actual treat, and never fill the ball completely. Likewise, never offer your dog a meal directly before placing him in the crate. Instead, allow about a half hour for digestion, so he can empty his bladder and bowels beforehand.

HOUSETRAINING

Housetraining can be one of the most daunting dog-training tasks. Although this isn't a process you can breeze through overnight, it does not have to be difficult either. All dogs—even littermates—are different when it comes to how quickly they catch on to housetraining, but there are certain steps that every owner can employ to help ensure quicker (and permanent) success.

Some people insist that English Cocker Spaniels are harder to housetrain than many other breeds, but this likely has more to do with the owner's approach to training than the breed's aptitude (or lack thereof) for learning. English Cockers are very intelligent dogs, and they love being praised for a job well done more than anything. When punishment is used with them, however, they can develop a stubborn resistance to accommodating their trainers. If this happens, expect the training process to last a long time.

Starting Off on the Right Foot

As soon as your puppy is old enough to come home, he will be ready to begin the housetraining process. The best way to anticipate the times when your puppy will need to eliminate is to establish a schedule and stick to it. A general guideline for determining how often your English Cocker will need to relieve himself is two hours for every eight weeks of age. An eight-week-old puppy will therefore need to eliminate every two hours and a four-month-old puppy every four hours. This reaches a reasonable limit by the time the dog is between five and six months old—no English Cocker Spaniel should ever be forced to hold his bladder for longer than five or six hours.

Scheduling your dog's meals can also help you predict his bowel movements. Most dogs need to void their bowels approximately 20 to 30 minutes after eating. If more than a half hour has passed, and your dog still hasn't eliminated, exercise may help speed the process.

A properly crate-trained dog will see his crate as a private, pleasant refuge.

There are several telltale signs that your English Cocker is looking for a place to eliminate: He may sniff around, circle, or pace back and forth. Occasionally, a dog will develop his own unique pre-elimination habit. If this is the case with your dog, simply make note of his individual signs and watch for them so that you can redirect him to the proper area whenever necessary.

Accidents Happen

If one thing is to be expected when it comes to housetraining, it is that your puppy will have accidents—although, in the beginning, there will be little that is truly "accidental" about them. When your puppy first arrives home, he will not know where he is supposed to relieve himself, so it's your job to show him. One effective way of doing this is by taking him to your chosen "potty spot"—a particular area of your backyard, for example. As the two-hour mark nears, place your English Cocker on his leash and bring him to this spot.

Introducing the Crate

When my husband and I recently brought home our new puppy, Damon, we allowed him to investigate his new crate for several days before ever even thinking of closing the door. We also purchased his kennel a few weeks before his arrival and placed it directly beside our other Cocker's crate as a way of showing her that a new dog would be entering the household. Whether she knew why it was there or not, I cannot say for certain, but she was definitely curious. Interestingly, she sniffed the entire exterior thoroughly as soon as it arrived, but never offered to set a single paw inside.

When Damon arrived, the crate was just another item in a vast new space to him, but as he noticed us toss toys inside, he began to venture in, too. He also noticed rather quickly that Molly readily entered the kennel next door, but he dared not cross the invisible boundary and enter himself. Each dog seemed to respect the other's space.

When the time came for closing the door, our breeder suggested using a treat ball to entertain the puppy when inside the crate. "Be careful to only offer this toy when he's in the crate, though," she warned, "or it won't have the effect that you want." The goal, of course, was to make Damon associate a fun toy that dispensed tasty treats with being inside his crate, which he did. In no time at all, he began running to his crate whenever he heard the sound of this illustrious toy.

I won't say that he never whimpered, but by only leaving him for short periods of time, and gradually increasing the duration, Damon transitioned to his crate wonderfully. Just weeks after joining our home, he began regularly going inside to chew his Nylabone or play with his fleece duck whenever the mood struck him. Unlike Molly, Damon does not usually seek out his crate as a napping spot (he prefers the sofa), but he readily responds whenever I tell him it's time to go to his crate. He no longer needs the treat ball, but I still like to leave the house on a positive note by offering each of my pups a small healthy treat while saying a quick goodbye.

If he has already eliminated inside the house, bring the poop (or wet paper towel from the clean-up) with you outdoors and place it on the ground. This will help show your dog that this is where he should be relieving himself instead. As he starts eliminating outside, you can simply leave his last bowel movement there as a reminder—as long as he's eliminating in your own yard, of course—and dispose of the older one each time, so the area doesn't become contaminated by compounding feces.

Although it may be tempting to scold your dog when he relieves himself in an inappropriate place, the best thing to say is actually nothing at all. Instead, praise your dog abundantly whenever he goes in the appropriate location. This will increase the chances of him repeating the desired behavior. Many English Cockers are capable of learning to eliminate on command —that is, they will relieve themselves faster upon their owners' instruction to "pee" or "poop" (or whatever word or phrase you choose to use for the activity). The way to teach this association is to say the word in an upbeat tone as soon as your dog begins relieving himself in the proper place. This should, of course, be followed with lavish praise. Be sure to wait for him to go before saying the word, though, or he won't be able to learn what it means.

You should *never* use physical punishment of any kind in response to housetraining accidents. Hitting a dog with a rolled-up newspaper or rubbing his nose in excrement does absolutely nothing to foster housetraining. It will, however, almost certainly damage your relationship with your English Cocker. Like children, animals should be treated with love and respect, not violence or humiliation.

Cleaning Up Accidents

As soon as you notice that your English Cocker has made a housetraining mistake, quietly remove him from visual range and then clean up the mess. Allowing your dog to watch you take care

Your dog requires frequent trips outside to eliminate— at least once every five hours for an adult English Cocker.

of his accident can offer the impression that his role is to make the messes and your job is to clean them up. At the moment, this may be closer to the truth than you'd like, but your English Cocker certainly doesn't have to know it.

Whenever cleaning a wetting accident from carpeting, always absorb the urine completely before scrubbing the area, or you will just be embedding any amount that is left behind further into the fibers. Once the area feels totally dry, be sure to use a product made specifically for cleaning pet odors, as this will help prevent your dog from revisiting the scene of the crime. (Even if you cannot smell a thing, I assure you that your English Cocker Spaniel will.) A number of such products are available at most pet supply stores, although some pet owners insist that plain white vinegar and water works equally well. No matter which product or homemade solution you use, avoid ammonia at all costs. Since canine urine contains a high concentration of this compound, cleaning with this ingredient will only encourage your dog to wet the area over and over again.

Outdoor Training

The majority of English Cocker Spaniel owners choose to train their dogs to eliminate outdoors, either in a specific area (a spot in their backyards, for example) or while walking around their neighborhoods. Certainly, no one enjoys handling animal excrement, but this method works best for those dog owners who prefer not to deal with it in their homes. With outdoor training there are no wet newspapers to change, no smelly litter box to clean, and no corner of your home that gets commandeered as a canine bathroom. Walking your dog as a prelude to elimination also offers the added benefits to both dog and owner of getting regular exercise and fresh air together.

If you do leave the confines of your backyard, be sure to bring along a disposable bag for cleanup. If you find the job of handling of your English Cocker's housetraining accidents distasteful, imagine the disdain of your neighbors when they unwittingly step in piles of feces left in front of their homes. Cleaning up after your dog is not only a common courtesy among neighbors, it is also the law.

During the first few weeks with your new English Cocker Spaniel puppy, it may seem that you are spending most of your

Are English Cocker Spaniels Easily Trained?

In a word, yes. Housetraining should begin as soon as you get your English Cocker puppy home, and he will learn quickly as long as you keep to the following points:

- Learn to recognize when the puppy is looking for a place to "go" (they will often sniff along the ground and circle as they look for the "right" spot).

- When you notice your dog's sign that he has to eliminate, take him straight outside and wait for him to relieve himself, using a key phrase such as "Hurry up!" or "Be quick." Praise him as soon as he has finished.

- Make meal times and trips outside to eliminate routine.

- Always take him to the same place to eliminate.

- At first, take him outside at least every two hours in daytime. He will also need to go out after meals, sleeping, or playing. As he grows up, he will be able to last for longer periods between visits outside. Adult dogs should have the chance to go outside at least every four hours.

(Courtesy of the Cocker Spaniel Club)

time together outside. Indeed, the initial schedule of taking your dog out every two hours can be a grueling one, but I cannot stress enough the importance of following this routine. Until your dog experiences at least some level of success with housetraining, your goal will be to anticipate his need to eliminate and get him to his potty spot before an accident occurs. By taking him out at the times he is most likely to eliminate, you increase his chances of success significantly. As soon as he begins to relieve himself outside, you will be able to start the real training—reinforcing the behavior with copious praise.

It is relatively easy to schedule your dog's meals around this two-hour routine, but one thing you cannot always plan is your puppy's nap time. Puppies tend to play hard and nap often, and they always seem to need to empty their bladders as soon as they wake up, so be sure to grab that leash at these times, too. Many pups need to eliminate after vigorous play sessions, as well.

LEASH TRAINING

Leash training is, sadly, one of the most overlooked parts of the training process for many dogs. With larger breeds, such as the Mastiff or Saint Bernard, an owner would hardly imagine skipping this important step, but for some reason many owners of more conservatively sized breeds seem to think that leash training is optional. Even if your English Cocker has a spacious, fenced backyard in which to run and play most of the time, there will still be times when he is expected to walk peaceably alongside you. Whether your dog is a puppy and seems more interested in grabbing and pulling at his leash than walking on it or his leash has never adorned his collared neck since he entered your home, the time to start the leash training process is now.

Start Early

Maybe, like some other new dog owners, you are planning to incorporate leash training into your routine later, when your puppy is a little older. Maybe your plan just doesn't include walking your dog in public for exercise, so teaching this elementary activity now seems a waste of your time and effort. I assure you that, in either situation, you will regret putting off until tomorrow what your English Cocker Spaniel can easily master today.

Even if you won't be walking your dog around the block every day, there are times when he must be on a leash. I know when I visit my dog's vet, often several other animals (cats as well as dogs) are waiting for their appointments with their owners. In this virtually unavoidable situation, leashes help keep everyone safe. Sure, I can carry my 22-pound (10 kg) Cocker almost anywhere,

Never punish your puppy for housetraining accidents—he'll only learn to fear and mistrust you.

but holding her still when she sees a Maltese, a black Lab, and two cats together in the same room is a whole new ball game.

Socialization is another area in which having leash-trained your dog is useful. Most of the best places to take your English Cocker—the park, the pet supply store, the beach—all require a dog to be kept on a leash.

By introducing the

leash as soon as your puppy arrives home, you will likely avoid such unpleasant problems as fear and aggression. You will also be able to start the training process while your dog is still small enough not to pull you around the neighborhood as he learns the proper way to walk alongside you instead. Even an adult English Cocker Spaniel may indeed be too small to pull you off your feet, but I know for a fact that a determined English Cocker *can* make you wonder for a moment if you have dislocated your shoulder.

Use It Often

In addition to starting early, you should make a point of using your dog's leash often—preferably every day. In the very beginning, this may mean simply attaching the leash to your English Cocker's collar and letting him walk around the house while wearing it. (For safety's sake, use baby gates or close doorways leading to stairways when doing this exercise, and keep an eye on your pup to make sure the leash doesn't catch on anything.) If your puppy appears apprehensive about wearing his leash, even indoors, start instead by leaving the leash out for him to approach and investigate on his own. Praise him generously whenever he makes an effort to check it out or spends any time tolerating wearing it.

Once you venture outside with your puppy on his leash, your next goal is to teach him how to walk without pulling. Initially, keep the sessions short—just a few minutes each day—and praise him for just walking alongside you. Keeping treats as lures can help keep your dog closer to your side if he tends to lag behind or pull forward. *Never* yank on his leash to keep him from pulling, though. In fact, if he tends to pull too strongly, you might want to change from a collar to a harness until he learns basic leash etiquette.

Once your dog seems to have mastered the concept of matching your pace, begin putting just a little pressure on the leash as you lead him in a direction of your choice. Again, praise your dog for complying. If you are using food rewards, be sure to only offer them

Occasionally, a dog who has previously mastered the housetraining process begins having accidents again for no apparent reason. If this happens to your English Cocker, make an appointment with his veterinarian to rule out a medical cause, such as a kidney problem or diabetes, since incontinence can be a warning sign of either condition. It is crucial that you make sure the problem is not physical before you decide how to approach the issue behaviorally.

when your dog is in the process of walking alongside, never when he is resisting the lead.

BASIC OBEDIENCE

The word "obedience" can sound like a menacing term. For some dog owners, just the mention of it inspires a harsh image of canine boot camp, complete with an angry drill sergeant. Fortunately, the reality isn't anything like this. Basic obedience training is not only a very practical step for almost any dog, but it is also very often an enjoyable undertaking for both dog and owner.

Many people are surprised to learn that obedience is far less about control than it is about communication and keeping your dog safe in almost any situation. The wider your dog's obedience vocabulary, the greater your chances will be that he listens to you when it matters most—in a dangerous situation. The process also focuses just as much on your own learning as your dog's, for obedience teaches human–canine communication. It also builds a strong foundation for all future learning.

If you are one of the people whose shoulders tense from just imagining your dog in an obedience class, you will be very pleased to know that obedience training can also be a lot of fun for both you and your pet. Like any type of dog training, obedience should always be a positive experience—centering on praise and accomplishment, never punishment. If you still feel uncomfortable taking part in an obedience class, however, many excellent books and videos are available that can help you teach your dog these basic commands in the privacy of your own home or backyard. I recommend at least giving a group setting a try, though. You will still need to make the effort to socialize your English Cocker

The sit *command is the basis for several other commands, and is one of the most important things you can teach your dog.*

Spaniel, after all, and classes like these are among the best means of doing so.

The most commonly taught obedience commands are *sit*, *down*, *stay*, and *come*. Teaching your dog just one of these commands can take time and a considerable amount of repetition, so be patient and consistent. As you follow up on what you have learned, remember to keep training sessions short. Begin working with your puppy in five-minute sessions three times a day. You can gradually increase the length to 10 minutes as he matures. By the time your dog is about eight months of age, he should be able to tolerate 15-minute sessions.

Sit

The *sit* command is the basis for many others, so it is a wonderful starting point for all future training. Even the youngest puppies are often capable of learning it.

Holding a treat in your closed hand, place the hand just above your dog's nose. As he moves his muzzle toward the treat, lift your hand slightly up and over his head and say the word "sit." This will naturally encourage your dog to shift his weight onto his haunches, moving himself into the sitting position. Once he sits, open your hand and offer the treat.

You should practice this command often and in a variety of places, so your dog is accustomed to sitting whenever and wherever you say the word. Be sure to spend at least some time working near the main entrance of your home, though, as this will make it easier to get him to comply even with the excitement of a visitor's arrival.

Down

The *down* command follows the *sit* command. It can be especially useful for helping your dog stay out of trouble, particularly when a person or another dog is approaching.

Beginning with your English Cocker in a sitting position, hold a treat in front of him and then slowly lower your hand in front of his paws as you say the word "down." When your dog lowers his body to get the treat, offer both the treat and verbal praise. Once he is easily moving into the down position as a response to your moving hand, start issuing the *down* command just before you show him the treat, and begin gradually limiting how far you lower or extend your hand. This will help wean your dog from depending on the visual cue.

Stay

Successfully learning the *stay* command can actually save your dog's life. Using this command whenever your doorbell rings, for example, can prevent him from running out the door when it opens. *Stay* can also be helpful when entertaining a visitor who is uncomfortable around dogs.

Once your dog can reliably sit when told, you can begin working on the *stay* command. Expect puppies to only remain still for just a second or two at first, but this duration will increase over time.

After instructing your pup to sit, raise your hand in a "stop" gesture while saying the word "stay." Take a step back, and then return to your dog, providing a treat and praise. Make sure he does not stand or move as you present the treat, as this will reward the wrong behavior.

When your dog is able to sit for a few seconds, begin gradually increasing both the number of steps you take away from him and the amount of time before offering the reward. Your ultimate goal is

Out of the Mouths of Pups

If your puppy tends to grab his leash in his mouth every time you hook it onto his collar, try offering him some other item to carry while walking instead. Sticks have always worked well with my Cockers, but a special toy may work as well or even better for yours. Although carrying his own leash may at first seem cute, it can interfere with your dog's leash training by providing him with an unnecessary point of leverage. If you wish to participate in advanced obedience training in the future, you will want to use the stick as only a temporary distraction from biting the leash, but if you don't, there is really no harm in allowing him to carry around this or another security item while out for walks.

Turning Your English Cocker Spaniel Into a Social Butterfly

Although socializing an English Cocker Spaniel puppy is one of the easiest parts of training, many owners skip this important task completely, mistakenly assuming that they just don't have enough time for it. The good news is that even dog owners who lead busy lives can usually fit socialization into their hectic schedules. You see, no class is available for socialization—the best course is simply including your dog in your own everyday activities.

My husband and I have found our son's Little League games to be an excellent opportunity for this. By keeping us company while we cheer the teams on, our Cocker puppy encounters other parents, children, and even other dogs. I always bring along some bite-sized treats for both friends and strangers to offer him. This helps teach our dog that dealing with people is an enjoyable activity. It also helps him get used to being in a crowded, noisy environment.

Other wonderful places to take a puppy for socialization include the beach, the park, the playground, and any advanced dog-training event that welcomes pets as part of the audience. You can also work on socializing your dog while taking daily walks by simply stopping to say hello to friendly neighbors and other people along the way.

for your dog to remain sitting and still for about a minute or longer with you at least 10 feet (3 m) away.

Come

The best way to start teaching your puppy the *come* command is by praising him whenever he does it naturally. If you spot your dog in the act of coming your way, say the word in an upbeat tone, followed by excessive praise. It is paramount that you never scold him after commanding him to come to you, no matter what he might have done. By following this very important rule, you will help ensure that your dog will always come to you when called, even when he may be in the midst of a scary situation.

When you are ready to begin working on this command more directly, make sure your dog is on a leash or that you have another individual available to gently lead him to you when necessary. Extendable leashes work extremely well for this purpose. Whether you prefer using a leash or a partner, you simply must have a way of getting your dog to follow the command if he doesn't promptly do so on his own.

Don't ignore any problem behaviors—most can be improved with training and patience.

PROBLEM BEHAVIORS

No dog owner would ever intentionally teach a dog such unpleasant behaviors as chewing or howling. Most people, after all, don't enjoy having their belongings destroyed or having to deal with angry landlords. If they don't know how to correct the problems, though, the end result will essentially be the same as if they had intentionally reinforced the behaviors all along. If your English Cocker Spaniel has adopted some objectionable pastimes, and you don't know how to change them, the worst thing you can do is ignore the situation. If you do, I assure you the problem will only get worse. Although some problems can be more difficult to solve than others, most can be improved as long as the owner is willing to be patient but persistent in addressing them.

Aggression

Canine aggression must never be tolerated. Although many factors can contribute to a dog's tendency to bite, there is no acceptable excuse. If there is only one situation for which obedience training is necessary, this is it. From their very first human experiences, puppies should never be allowed to bite—not even playfully. Teaching your dog that you are his leader is the most important step in correcting aggressive behavior. If your dog is biting, it may also be wise to consider details such as where your

The come *command can save your dog's life in an emergency situation.*

dog sleeps, when he is fed, and what games you play with him, and how these things may be affecting your dog's perception of his place in the family.

If your English Cocker Spaniel has assumed the alpha role in your household and uses aggressive behavior toward family members as a means of retaining this position, this is a true emergency. Consult your veterinarian, a canine obedience instructor or dog trainer, or an animal behaviorist immediately for advice on how to solve this very serious problem. If the problem is ignored, you could be faced with a lawsuit, or worse, the unimaginable possibility of being legally forced to euthanize your dog.

First, talk to your veterinarian. Often, changing just one part of your strategy can easily solve a problem you thought was much more complicated, and your vet may be able to identify the one part of the solution that has eluded you. Your vet's advice may be to enroll your dog in a basic obedience-training program or to consult a professional dog trainer, and these suggestions may indeed lead to a solution to the problem.

Chewing

Inappropriate chewing can have many possible reasons behind it. Teething, anxiety, boredom, and lack of exercise are all potential causes. To avert your dog from using your personal property as chew toys, provide him with a variety of acceptable items for chewing instead. Toys that present the opportunity for

stimulation—such as balls that release treats upon manipulation—can also be helpful in distracting your dog from feasting on your belongings.

Teach your dog a command such as *drop it* or *leave it* for those times you catch him chewing anything unacceptable. Avoid the temptation to give him an item he has already damaged. Although you may have no further use for it, allowing your English Cocker to keep it will only further confuse him as to what is and isn't fair game. For this reason, also avoid giving your dog old shoes or clothing as toys. When he begins chewing an improper item, remove it from his possession and offer one of his own chew toys as a replacement. Praise him if he accepts the substitute.

Excessive Barking or Howling

The best method for reducing excessive barking is good old-fashioned distraction. Music can serve as a wonderful buffer if noises tend to prompt your English Cocker's barking. Placing his crate away from outside walls or windows where people and other sounds can easily be heard can also help. Socializing your dog may help if he barks mostly when you entertain visitors within your home. In this case, providing your dog with a special treat that he receives only when visitors are present may be effective.

English Cockers are very good at alerting their owners to the presence of strangers, so this may be the key factor in your dog's barking problem. (I am convinced that my two Cockers think they own the sidewalk in front of our home.) You will not be able to completely stop your dog from barking when he hears a suspicious noise—and you may actually want him to serve this watchdog role. This doesn't mean that you want prolonged barking, however. In this case, you should teach your dog the *enough* command.

To teach this command, you must first teach the *speak* command.

Provide your English Cocker with plenty of suitable chew toys to reduce the likelihood of problematic chewing.

Do this by issuing the command as you knock on any hard surface, hopefully encouraging your dog to bark in response to the noise. Once your English Cocker learns to speak upon command, begin saying the word "enough" as soon as there is a break in the barking, rewarding him immediately for stopping. The timing of

the command is crucial, as you want to issue the command as soon as your dog stops barking; otherwise, you will be rewarding the wrong behavior.

When your English Cocker informs you of an approaching visitor or other noise, praise him for bringing the sound to your attention. Once you acknowledge the situation, say, "Enough." As soon as your dog stops barking, offer a reward. This will ultimately teach him that bringing a noise to your attention is acceptable, but continued barking is not.

Separation Anxiety

Howling or extended barking when your dog is left at home alone can be a trickier problem. Domestic dogs often howl only when prompted by a specific sound (such as a siren), but in the wild, dogs howl as a means of bringing their pack together. If excessive howling or barking only occurs when your dog is left alone, this may signal a deeper problem of separation anxiety. If ignored, separation anxiety can further present itself in the form of destructive chewing, housetraining regression, and sometimes even self-mutilation. One indication that you are dealing with an issue of separation is if you offer your dog a treat when you leave and frequently return to see that it has remained uneaten.

The most common underlying causes of canine separation anxiety are confusion, fear, and stress. A variety of issues could be at the root of the problem: Perhaps your dog was taken from his mother too early, a common occurrence at puppy mills. Maybe your dog's previous owner abandoned him at a shelter, leaving him especially fearful of your leaving him now. Maybe you have returned to working full time after taking a few weeks off to spend with your new puppy. Again, this is a situation in which teaching basic obedience skills can help your dog become a more confident, less anxious being—the key to reversing this condition.

Spend time with your English Cocker Spaniel regularly. Take him for walks often; regular exercise can significantly reduce his stress. Provide him with a crate for security, and follow the protocol of slowly introducing it while you *are* at home. If you cannot seem to correct the problem, consider enrolling your English Cocker in daycare or having someone else care of him when you cannot be there. Even having a dog walker stop by during the day may offer just enough of a break from the solitude to help your dog cope with

Exictable and Submissive Urination

Many dogs, English Cocker Spaniels included, tend to leak a bit of urine when excited or when in the presence of a person they consider to be a superior dog. In either situation, remedial housetraining is not necessary. Both these problems can usually be managed by making a few small changes to your household routine, such as postponing the greeting process after returning home until your dog has had a chance to calm down and relieve himself in the appropriate spot.

being alone while you are away.

FINDING AN ANIMAL BEHAVIOR SPECIALIST

The work of an animal behaviorist involves observing, interpreting, and modifying animal behavior so she can help clients solve their pets' most serious problem behaviors. The biggest difference between behaviorists and other animal trainers or instructors is the severity of the problems they address. Dog trainers and obedience instructors help owners prevent negative behaviors before they become issues. They may also work with owners to correct mild problem behaviors. Behaviorists, on the other hand, deal with more substantial matters.

The advice of a behaviorist may be necessary if your dog suffers from acute anxiety or phobias, aggression, or other behavioral disorders. In most situations, conventional trainers are not qualified to deal with these issues. Even a veterinarian may not be able to help in many cases.

Like dog trainers and obedience instructors, behaviorists do not need any form of licensing to do their work, so careful selection is a must. Although a certification process does exist, it is still fairly new and not well known; currently, only a limited number of certified behaviorists exist. You can find a directory of these individuals at www.animalbehavior.org. What is most important

Contact an animal behaviorist if your English Cocker exhibits problem behaviors that are difficult or impossible for you to address on your own.

is that you are comfortable with the individual you choose, but you should also seek a person with a certain level of education and experience dealing with animals, particularly small dogs. A degree in some form of psychology or zoology is a definite advantage. The person should also possess dog-training knowledge and experience. References from former clients are good, but recommendations from veterinarians and humane societies are even better. If you cannot find a certified behaviorist in your area on your own, these are the best resources that may lead to one.

7

ADVANCED TRAINING
and ACTIVITIES
With Your English Cocker Spaniel

A standing joke in our house is that, although our Cocker Spaniel Molly is a beautiful girl, she's definitely no lady. The first to jump into the fray of a good old-fashioned game of "Let's Get Daddy," she is also usually the last to surrender. Her half-brother Damon will always join in on the fun at least for a little while, but truth be told he is much happier cuddling with Mom than rolling around on the floor and taking the chance of ending up under one of Molly's deceivingly delicate-looking paws.

Like Molly, many Cockers thrive on physical interaction as a means of exercise and play, but informal games like this one are just part of the fun that awaits them. If your English Cocker seems to enjoy performing for others, there are several organized activities both you and your dog may enjoy doing together. If your dog is athletic like Molly, agility may be a wonderful pastime. If, conversely, your dog is more ladylike (or gentlemanly), perhaps obedience or conformation would suit the two of you better. Does your dog have a great nose? Tracking just might be for him.

Whatever activity you may choose, the rewards go much deeper than ribbons and titles. While training and competing, you will meet some wonderful people, your dog will build a new level of self-esteem, and the bond between you will strengthen in a way you have probably never before experienced. More than anything else, the time you spend together working toward your goals will be something you cherish for the rest of your lives together.

Like people, dogs enjoy having something rewarding to do with their time. English Cockers in particular love learning, and there is no better form of learning than an activity that makes their owners proud. Your dog may get great satisfaction from his daily walks with you or from spending time with the rest of his family, but what does he do when it rains all week? Or when everyone else in the house seems to have gone separate ways for the afternoon? Advanced training activities offer your English Cocker a pastime of his own, a date that can be kept no matter what the weather, and the added benefits of human and canine socialization.

CANINE GOOD CITIZEN PROGRAM

One of the best platforms for any advanced training activity, and truly an accomplishment within itself, is the completion of the American Kennel Club's (AKC) Canine Good Citizen (CGC) program. A certification series begun in 1989, the CGC program stresses responsible pet ownership by rewarding dogs who display good manners both at home and in the community. Those interested may attend the CGC training program, an optional class offered to owners and their dogs, before taking a detailed 10-step test. Certificates are awarded upon completion.

The CGC program focuses primarily on a dog's obedience skills and temperament, but it also stresses the importance of a serious owner commitment. All owners are required to sign a Responsible Dog Owners Pledge before taking the test. This unique document states that the owner agrees to effectively care for her dog for the rest of the animal's life. It also encompasses such important areas as health and safety, exercise and training, and basic quality of life. It even addresses such community-based issues as agreeing to clean up after your dog in public and never allowing him to infringe on the rights of others.

A dog who earns a Canine Good Citizen certificate is recognized as a responsible member of his community.

A dog who passes this valuable examination receives an AKC certificate complete with the CGC logo embossed in gold. CGC certification can also be useful to your dog in many other areas of advanced training. A dog worthy of the revered title of Canine Good Citizen is considered a responsible member of his community, a community that includes both people and dogs he already knows and all of those he will encounter in the future.

Although dogs of any age may participate in the CGC program, puppies must be at least old enough to have had all necessary immunizations. To ensure that your dog's certification is reliable, it's strongly recommended that younger dogs who pass the test get retested as adults, since temperaments and abilities can possibly change

Good Citizen Dog Scheme

In the UK, the Kennel Club (KC) offers the Good Citizen Dog Scheme, a certification series including four levels of recognition—Puppy Foundation, Bronze, Silver, and Gold. Like the AKC's Good Citizen Program, the Good Citizen Dog Scheme rewards well-behaved and trained dogs in the community. As a dog advances from one level to the next, new concepts are added to the test with increasing levels of difficulty. More than 1,600 organizations throughout England, Scotland, Wales, and Northern Ireland offer Good Citizen training classes. Since 1992, more than 80,000 dogs have passed the Bronze test alone.

A handbook entitled "The Good Citizen Dog Scheme Guidelines" is available for a nominal fee from the KC website.

during this formative period. All breeds (as well as mixed breeds) are welcome in the program.

GAMES

The benefits of creative play are numerous. Unlike more monotonous forms of exercise, such as walking or running, a game that provides both a mental and physical workout can increase your dog's intelligence, lower his stress level, and even sharpen skills he uses in other, more organized activities. Additionally, games are just plain fun for both dogs and owners.

When my husband and I were first married, we rented a second-floor apartment from a rather serious man who lived downstairs from us with his adopted Greyhound. One afternoon when I returned home from work, I opened the gate and found my landlord posed guardedly behind the mammoth pine tree that occupied our backyard. He immediately placed his right index finger to his lips and mouthed the words "hide-and-seek." I then looked to the Greyhound racing frantically around the yard. When the dog saw me, she stopped for just a moment as if to say, "Um, we're in the middle of a game here," and then returned at once to her search. It didn't take her long to realize, though, that what had first captured my attention was the object of her game. As soon as she found him, her owner jumped forward and smiled, looking only slightly embarrassed and said out loud to me, "Nice day, isn't it?"

This is only one (albeit heartwarming) example of a game you can play with your own canine best friend. Just be sure to limit

Staying Ahead of the Game

Always allow your dog to be the seeker when you play hide and seek together. Doing so could even save his life in the future, should complying with the come command become a serious matter—if he escapes your yard and runs toward the street, for example. By encouraging your dog to hide from you—even during play—you could inadvertently reinforce the behavior, which could be extremely dangerous in emergency situations.

yourself to indoor hiding spots unless, like our former landlord, you have a fenced-in yard. If your English Cocker has already learned basic obedience commands, this can also be a great way to practice the commands *sit, stay*, and *come*. If either of you tires of the same old game, try hiding a treat and having your dog search for that instead. Just remember to always reward your dog when he wins the game!

Some dogs, particularly those who like to jump, enjoy chasing bubbles immensely. For them, a single bottle of non-toxic bubbles is all you need for an entire afternoon of fun. If the wind is blowing, making other activities *less* pleasant, it will only make your game of bubbles more exciting.

Other games commonly played with dogs include fetch, Frisbee, and ball. Many owners also like to create variations of these games or invent entirely new ones for their pets. For example, maybe you would like to teach your English Cocker to play basketball. All you need is a small, lightweight ball and some type of receptacle—a child's adjustable basketball hoop, a five-gallon bucket, or even a stack of old tires could serve this purpose. Remember, games are about imagination, so the possibilities are as endless as yours.

OBEDIENCE

For many dog owners, advanced training in obedience begins with a relatively casual level of involvement—taking your English Cocker Spaniel to a basic obedience class as a puppy, for instance, or even working with your dog privately to teach him a few commands you think he should know. In many cases, though, both dog and owner discover that this seemingly stoic style of training can actually be a really fun pastime for all involved. Advanced obedience training, when properly implemented, is simply higher education for your English Cocker Spaniel.

The first step toward competing in formal obedience is training your dog. You may choose to do this independently at home or with the assistance of a trained instructor, either alone or with a class. You dog will need to know *sit*, *stay*, *come*, and *heel*. At the entry levels of competition, your dog will need to perform these commands promptly and in the presence of other dogs and their owners. He must also stand for a judge's inspection. Once he advances through the various levels of competition, the duration of time he will be expected to stay, for example, will be extended, and he will also need to perform certain commands while off leash.

In obedience competition, the first class you will enter is the novice class, also called the Companion Dog (CD) class. This beginning level focuses on demonstrating the skills of a good canine companion: heeling both on and off leash at different speeds, coming when called, and staying for fixed periods of time while also remaining still and quiet with a group of other dogs. Your English Cocker will also be required to stand for a basic physical examination by the judges.

Next is the open class. This second tier of obedience is also called the Companion Dog Excellent (CDX) class. In this level, your dog repeat many of the same exercises from the novice level, but off leash and for longer periods of time. Jumping and retrieving tasks are also included in this phase.

Your English Cocker is likely to enjoy playing fetch with his favorite toys.

The utility level, which provides your English Cocker with a Utility Dog (UD) title, is for dogs nearing the top of their obedience game. In this stage, your English Cocker will perform more difficult exercises, complete with hand signals, as well as scent discrimination tasks. Once he can perform at this level, he can go on to pursue the highest possible titles of Obedience Trial Champion (OTCh) and Utility Dog Excellent (UDX). Both are prestigious titles and not easily nor quickly achieved.

Like the CGC program, obedience is considered by many English Cocker enthusiasts to be a great foundation for many other canine activities. Maybe your ultimate plan is for your English Cocker to become a therapy dog, or perhaps you just want to participate in a fun weekend pastime with your dog, with any rewards being just an added bonus. Whatever obedience means to you, bear in mind that succeeding does not mean that your dog must earn all available titles. As with any activity, there is nothing wrong with striving toward your next goal, but the most important thing is enjoying the road that leads there. Any owner of an English Cocker who earns a CDX or UD title should be proud, as these are reputable accomplishments.

SHOWING (CONFORMATION)

Dog shows, also called conformation events, evaluate just how closely the entrants match their breed's standard, an indication of an animal's ability to produce quality puppies. Showing is in fact a means of evaluating breeding stock; therefore, spayed and neutered dogs may not participate. The second smallest member of the sporting group (the American Cocker is the smallest), the English Cocker Spaniel is no stranger to the ring. The breed has been formally shown for more than a century.

Selecting an Instructor

The most important decision you make along the road of obedience is your choice of instructors. Though several different trainers can be equally competent, it is always best to select the one with whom both you and your dog feel the most comfortable. Credentials and experience matter significantly, but never underestimate the power of a good relationship or a true rapport with animals. This is a situation in which your instincts, as well as your dog's, matter just as much as anything you can read about on paper.

Dogs entered into conformation events are evaluated based on how well they conform to their breed's standard.

Before an English Cocker Spaniel, or any breed, can be entered into a conformation show, he must meet certain criteria. A complete list of rules and regulations governing eligibility may be obtained from the AKC, but basic guidelines require that your dog be a purebred English Cocker Spaniel, AKC-registered, and at least six months old.

How Dog Shows Work

Shows can range in size and variety from small, local specialty events to national all-breed shows with more than 3,000 entrants. Even if you have no plans of ever showing your English Cocker, attending a large-scale AKC conformation event can be an amazing experience for any true dog fancier. At no other place will you ever see so many different breeds all in one place, many of which you may never have seen previously.

Breeds are divided into seven groups: sporting dogs, hounds, working dogs, terriers, toys, nonsporting dogs, and herding dogs. Each dog is then placed in one of five classes: puppy, novice, bred by exhibitor, American-bred, and open. Males are always judged first. Once an English Cocker Spaniel is judged Best of Breed, that dog then goes on to represent the breed in the group competition.

What to Wear

It is understandable to want to look your best when showing your dog. Judges and spectators usually dress up for shows, so it would seem logical that matching their standards of attire would be the best way to show respect for the event. While this is certainly true, it is equally important for handlers to dress appropriately for the ring. The right clothes help you show your dog to his best advantage.

Select clothing that reflects both class and comfort. You will need clothes that allow you to bend or kneel as necessary, and this can be difficult in a restrictive suit or ladylike skirt. There is certainly nothing wrong with wearing a suit, as long as it allows you to move freely about the ring. Pantsuits and split skirts are freeing alternatives to dresses and more traditional skirts for female handlers. A versatile choice for male handlers is a pair of trousers paired with a well-tailored blazer.

Avoid bold prints or clothing that clashes with your dog's features. Colors and fabrics should not detract from your dog's appearance, but contrast is often advantageous. Remember, your English Cocker Spaniel should be the one drawing everyone's attention.

From a novice perspective, it may seem that many of the dogs belonging to each breed look nearly identical. To the well-trained eye of an AKC judge, however, the differences can be significant. Judges look at every nuance of an individual dog to compare him to his breed standard. All entrants are carefully scrutinized in this way, and those dogs with obvious faults are eliminated, allowing the best specimens to rise to the top of the competition.

Getting Started

If you are interested in participating in conformation events, begin by first attending shows as a spectator. If the grooming area is open to the public, introduce yourself to the other English Cocker Spaniel owners there and ask if they would mind telling you about their experiences with showing. Although this is a competitive environment, many extremely kind and outgoing people are involved in the activity, are willing to help newcomers, and also enjoy sharing their enthusiasm for the breed with other kindred spirits.

In addition to exhibitors, vendors and information booths can also be valuable resources. If you are still considering purchasing your first English Cocker Spaniel, these are all wonderful starting points. Most of the breeders at AKC-sanctioned events are among the very best and can help point you toward a show-quality dog, if this is what you are seeking.

If you have already purchased your dog, consider joining an English Cocker Spaniel club. You will likely find that the organization offers classes for conformation training. Entering this sport and absorbing all the necessary information can be overwhelming. By taking it slow and learning as much as you can, you will help ensure a positive experience for both you and your dog.

Like other advanced training activities, showing requires great discipline on behalf of both dog and handler, but many people involved find it to be a labor of love. Showing English Cocker Spaniels can serve as a gateway to endless learning about this breed, wonderful friends who share your affinity for English Cockers, and an opportunity to strengthen your bond with your special pet.

Showing in the US and England

Although the showing process in Great Britain is relatively similar to that in the US, the road to championship is considerably different in the two countries. While the US uses a point system, the UK does not. Instead, judges award dogs with Challenge

If you plan to show your dog, attend a few conformation events as a spectator first and ask participants about their experiences.

The AKC encourages older children to participate in all kinds of advanced training as junior handlers. Although separate classes exist for juniors in conformation, juniors who handle dogs in agility, obedience, and tracking can obtain the same titles and awards as adult handlers.

Certificates. It is left up to the judge to decide how many dogs are worthy of this honor, so the overall number of entrants is somewhat irrelevant. Competition can be fierce, though, with shows often extending over several days each.

To obtain championship status, a dog must receive three Challenge Certificates from three different judges. One of these certificates must be awarded after the dog is 12 months old.

For many years, criticism was made that Challenge Certificates were being given out far too often, and that less than completely deserving dogs have received them. As a means of ensuring proper understanding of the criteria, the Kennel Club General Committee changed the wording of the official regulations for this award, effective January 1, 2005.

Another difference is the focused area of expertise of English judges compared to American judges. In England, judges who specialize in one particular breed are far more common. Since they have had such vast experience with the dogs they breed (or have bred in the past), these judges are considered the best authorities on that breed by the KC. An AKC judge is much more likely to judge several different breeds, having accumulated knowledge of them all without necessarily breeding all of them personally.

SPORTS

Agility

The sport of agility was developed in England in the 1970s. Resembling equestrian jumping competitions, canine agility courses consist of similar obstacles, but they are built to a smaller scale. One thing that certainly isn't downsized, however, is the fun. Agility competitions have quickly become an amazingly popular pastime all over the world, for both participants and a mass of mesmerized onlookers. As handlers run alongside their dogs, the canine athletes make their way over colorful bars, vaulted walks, and seesaws. Keep watching, and you will see the same dogs dash through A-frames, suspended tires, and tunnels. Handlers may assist their pups by offering hand signals, verbal commands, or both.

If your energetic English Cocker puppy seems destined for this activity, you will have a few months to attend some events and work with your dog informally before making a final decision. Unlike obedience, a dog must be 12 months old to compete in agility. Although dogs must be physically fit for either activity, agility is considerably more strenuous on a dog's body than obedience. Because a puppy's growing bones and ligaments are weaker than an adult's, the potential for injury is lessened substantially by waiting this reasonable amount of time.

You can, of course, start introducing your dog to agility obstacles at any age. Encouraging a young dog to run through chutes or tunnels, for instance, may very well help him avoid any fears of these objects later. Do avoid any tasks involving jumping, though, until he is older. If you would like to at least familiarize your puppy with bar jumps, you may simple lay one bar on the ground and have him walk over it instead of jumping over it.

All dog breeds (and mixes) are welcome to participate in agility. This is ultimately where the similarities of agility and obedience end, however. One distinctive difference that many agility enthusiasts tout as an advantage of their pastime is the amount of handler involvement allowed in this sport: Agility handlers are permitted to talk to their dogs, redirect them verbally, or cheer them on at any time.

Setup and Equipment

Every activity has both advantages as well as disadvantages. In the case of agility, the biggest drawbacks are the cost of setup and the space the multiple pieces of equipment demand. It can also be relatively time consuming to assemble a backyard course for practice, especially if you need to disassemble it when you are finished so that the space can be used for something else.

In some areas, owners who don't have the resources to practice the sport at home can rent entire agility rings by the hour or the day. In the beginning, you can also use certain makeshift items in place of more expensive equipment. A child's play tunnel, for example, can serve as an affordable alternative to a regulation tunnel for a dog new to agility. A home extension ladder can help teach a dog to walk within a narrow space or to train him to focus his attention forward. Once you have determined that your English Cocker is well suited to agility, you should then make a point of transitioning to conventional equipment so that he can acclimate to any subtle changes that could make a difference in his future performance in the ring. (Any item you use should also be completely safe for your dog.)

Matters of Opinion

Although all conformation judges refer to the same written standard for the relevant breed, opinion must always play a part. Judging is by definition a subjective activity, since even breed standards are open to interpretation. A competing English Cocker Spaniel may have what his owner deems the quintessential topline, whereas a judge might only see this feature as being within the range of acceptability — and much less apparent than the dog's tail, which he carries just a bit too low. In the ring, it is only the judge's opinion that matters, and very often it is just that — an opinion.

Hunting and Field Trials

If your English Cocker Spaniel has retained the breed's love of the hunt, field trials may offer him an exciting opportunity to get back to his roots. Styled after traditional game hunts, these exciting events provide a unique chance for owners and dogs to compete together in this oldest canine sport. An individual event may be open to multiple sporting breeds or limited to just one.

Certainly, English Cockers can still hunt in the old-fashioned way. The purpose of field trial clubs is to prepare sporting dogs for either activity, so a dog trained through one of these organizations should be capable of vying for titles *and* putting food on his owner's table.

If you think you might enjoy competing in this sport with your English Cocker, get him involved when he is as young as possible. You can have a puppy tested for so-called "birdiness" before deciding if this is the dog for you. (Many kennels breed with this hunting purpose in mind; you will probably have the best luck finding an English Cocker well suited to this activity by purchasing

An energetic English Cocker is an excellent candidate for the sport of agility.

a dog from one of these breeders.) An English Cocker Spaniel can start training as early as just eight weeks old. It is not unusual to see a pup this age training alongside an older, more seasoned counterpart, each carrying a wing as they proudly retrieve a bird together.

Like formal obedience trials, field trials offer several levels of competition, with a respective point system for each, but the specifics are a bit more complicated for this activity. The number of other breeds involved in a particular event and even an individual dog's age, for example, can play important roles. A good breeder experienced in this sport should be able to help guide you through the process.

Take a Hike!

Walking and running are two of the healthiest forms of exercise for both people and dogs. What's more, taking part requires no fancy equipment or major expense. You can enjoy either activity virtually anywhere,

The Overscheduled English Cocker Spaniel

While no rules bar a dog from competing in multiple advanced training activities, you may want to limit the number of organized hobbies in which you and your English Cocker participate for the simple sake of not over-committing either one of you. Pastimes such as conformation events and agility trials demand a great amount of dedication from their participants, both in and out of the ring. Although the actual competitions may normally be held only on weekends, you will need to spend a considerable amount of time preparing for them.

Even if show dates don't present a scheduling conflict, you must be practical in deciding how many activities you can realistically juggle. This number will vary for different people. For some owners, two activities may be too many, while others might easily be able to handle two or even three without a problem. What is important is that these events remain pleasurable and don't turn into obligations that present more stress than enjoyment.

Watch your dog's reactions as you expose him to different activities, and pursue those that you both seem to enjoy most. Being involved also doesn't have to mean attending each and every event. It may take a little more time for your dog to earn a title at this slower pace, but the most important title he will ever have is that of your much-loved pet.

anytime. When your dog walks or runs, his body utilizes and strengthens various muscles, and he experiences an increase in heart rate, a basic requirement of any cardiovascular activity. Sensible precautions must be taken with either pastime, though, to help prevent the dangers of physical injury, overexertion, and dehydration.

Walking can serve as a sensible introduction to a more intense exercise program, such as running, or it can be a worthwhile activity in its own right. Ideal for dogs of virtually all fitness levels, walking strikes many people as the quintessential human–canine pastime. It requires no instruction, it provides both dogs and owners with a regular dose of fresh air and sunshine, and it can be adjusted to fit into almost any routine.

Running (or jogging) with your English Cocker Spaniel, on the other hand, is an activity that demands a bit more preparation and a lot more vigilance. A dog who has never before run for any length of time, for example, needs to be introduced to the pursuit gradually—starting with only very short distances in the beginning and progressively increasing them. Just because your dog can run around with you in the backyard for what seems like hours on end does not mean he can keep up with you on a genuine five-mile run with no practical experience.

When running, always be on the lookout for signs that your dog needs a break. These can range from subtle (panting excessively and slowing down) to more obvious (increased salivation and outright stopping to sit down). If your dog tells you he needs to rest, honor his request by finding the nearest patch of shade for a respite period. Also, never run without taking along water for both you and your dog.

If your English Cocker is overweight, you should discuss the prospect of running together with your veterinarian, who may likely suggest postponing vigorous exercise until your dog's weight is down to a more reasonable level. In the meantime, grab your dog's leash, don your walking shoes, and get on the road to better health by putting one foot in front of the other.

Tracking

Whenever I take my Cockers for a walk, I am reminded of their innate ability to track scents. We can't even get to the end of our street without making several stops along the way—"getting their e-mail," as my mother whimsically refers to this ritual. Like other breeds, English Cocker Spaniels possess an acute sense of smell that human beings can hardly fathom, for dogs can detect odors at concentrations nearly 100 million times lower than we can. Imagine what our own walks would be like if we had this amazing capability!

English Cockers who have inherited their ancestors' hunting skills may enjoy participating in field trials.

Some English Cocker Spaniels seem to relish this gift more than others. Perhaps these dogs have an even more highly developed sense of smell than others, or maybe, like people, these English Cockers have learned to rely on this sense more so than other dogs in learning about their environments. It has been explained that most people are either visual or audio learners. A visual learner tends to remember things better once they have been written on a chalkboard, for instance, whereas an audio learner will be more likely to retain information that has been repeated multiple times. It would make sense that certain dogs excel at remembering things they have smelled with a similar aptitude.

The art of tracking has been around for as long as dogs have had noses, but organized tracking events are considerably younger. A vital part of working trials, competitive tracking is also known as "nosework". With a strong history for flushing game birds, the English Cocker Spaniel seems predestined to excel at this activity.

A sport that was once limited to fields and open spaces, competitive tracking is now also conducted in such urban areas as industrial zones, office parks, and even college campuses. The valuable skills honed through this contemporary canine sport can even be used for locating lost human beings or other animals in emergency situations.

THERAPY WORK

If you've ever had a pet, you know the uncanny ability most animals possess to raise their owners' spirits even on their worst days. In my opinion, this is especially true of dogs. They don't judge you, they don't hold grudges, and they don't even notice if you look your absolute worst. They just want to be with you. By sharing something as seemingly simple as their company, they can lighten your load and make all the stresses of everyday life seem just a little less important.

Because of their history as hunting dogs, English Cockers can make excellent trackers.

Therapy dogs take this natural gift a step further. In addition to offering their therapeutic companionship to their own beloved families, these animals, along with their thoughtful owners, share their time and love with other people who, for various reasons, can also benefit from a similar lift. Visiting hospitals, nursing homes, and other places where people are facing difficult situations, therapy dogs make a difference by merely doing what they do best—being dogs.

Keeping Your Cocker Cool

Since so many canine sporting events are held during the hottest months of the year, always come prepared. Keep your dog in a well-ventilated crate or exercise pen, preferably in the shade, until his time to compete arrives. He should also always have access to plenty of fresh drinking water. When allowed, fans are an excellent way to keep the airflow going.

In the event that your English Cocker Spaniel becomes overwhelmed by the heat and humidity, keep a few cold, damp towels in a nearby cooler. They shouldn't be too cold, however—don't shock your dog's system with ice or ice-cold water. Most importantly, if you suspect that your dog is suffering from heat exhaustion or heatstroke, get him to a vet as quickly as possible. The show may go on without you, but no title is worth risking your English Cocker Spaniel's health.

I've always thought that the concept of bringing dogs and people together in this way was an admirable undertaking, but I recently learned firsthand what a difference these dogs truly make. My father had been hospitalized, and my mother and I were waiting for him to return to his room after a lengthy procedure when a retired couple arrived at the door with a gorgeous German Shepherd. They told us his name was Olbs vom Huhnegrab— a/k/a Max—and asked if we'd like him to visit with us.

Since our minds were so affixed on my father and his illness, we said they were welcome to come in, but that the patient was not there at the moment. Of course, the couple immediately explained that Max was there to see everyone, patients and families alike.

At first I felt a little guilty petting this magnificent creature. I worried that I was taking up time he could be spending with patients who needed him much more than I did, but now I realize that his visit meant just as much to me as it did to anyone else that day. While talking to Max and his owners, my mother and I were able to relax just a little and focus our attention on something positive for the very first time that entire day. When they moved on to the next room, we felt more hopeful and were looking forward to telling my dad about the visit. The entire interaction lasted only minutes, but its effects helped carry us through the next two hours until my father finally returned from surgery.

When most people think of working dogs, German Shepherds like Max often spring to mind. While this is certainly one of the most popular breeds utilized for many important jobs, therapy work (like many other canine vocations) is open to all breeds (or breed mixes). Like countless other breeds, English Cocker Spaniels can make excellent therapy dogs.

If you think your English Cocker may have what it takes to become a therapy dog, you will need to have your dog certified before you are able to begin volunteering. Therapy Dogs International, Inc. (TDI), which was founded in 1976, certifies, insures, and registers therapy dogs so that they may visit health care facilities. The first requirement of TDI is certification as a CGC. Although this will not ensure your dog a place in a therapy program, the social skills necessary for this achievement are an excellent indicator that a dog is a good candidate for therapy work. If your dog fails his CGC test the first time around, don't despair; he can still go on to take it again. Dogs who are poorly suited for this activity are usually red-flagged fairly quickly, but it may take a bit more time to make sure that other applicants are indeed the right dogs for the job, so try to be as patient as possible.

You may find that your dog has an affinity for a certain part of the population. Maybe he seems to particularly enjoy the company of children, senior citizens, or mentally disabled people. If this is the case, I strongly recommend indulging this fascination, as members of this group will likely mirror your dog's inexplicable rapport with them. Therapy work is about making people feel good, but your English Cocker Spaniel will also be enriched by the lives he touches through this noble activity.

An English Cocker with the proper temperament and socialization may excel at therapy work.

HEALTH

of Your English Cocker Spaniel

What do you think is the most important aspect of your English Cocker Spaniel's good health? His genetic background? His diet? Maybe his veterinarian? Or how about making sure he gets enough exercise? While these are all vital parts of keeping your English Cocker in tip-top shape, the most significant factor is the common denominator—you. While you may not possess all the knowledge and expertise of a veterinarian, you are the person responsible for making the majority of the decisions that maintain your English Cocker's physical and mental well-being.

From the moment you select your puppy, you assume the role of his primary caregiver. You are the person who comes home to your dog every night, who takes him for his routine veterinary visits, and who notices immediately when something just doesn't seem right. Indeed, you are the person on whom your dog depends to do the research, make the calls, and keep the appointments. In this way, you affect his health more than any other individual in his life: By providing your dog with good health care—a lifelong commitment encompassing all of these tasks and more—you are ensuring that his life will be a long and happy one.

SELECTING A VETERINARIAN

Your English Cocker Spaniel's veterinarian should be someone who has a natural affinity for animals (dogs in particular), someone who listens to your concerns and addresses them with respect and understanding, and someone you trust with the care of your pet. Specific knowledge of the English Cocker breed is also helpful, as is a good rapport with your dog. Although this may sound like a mighty tall order, many extremely caring and capable vets out there will fit the bill. Unfortunately, there are also some mediocre, and worse, substandard veterinarians out there. Discerning the good ones from the bad is one of the most important tasks you will face as a dog owner.

Often, you may not be certain that you have chosen the best vet for your dog *until* a health problem arises. While you hope that you never have to experience one, a medical crisis instantly distinguishes the best vets from the rest. There are, however, several ways to evaluate a caregiver before you even bring your new puppy home. The very worst time to start looking for a vet is when your dog is already sick, so getting this big decision out of the way early is imperative.

Get Recommendations

Like so many other things relating to your English Cocker's care, one of the best places to find a good recommendation for a veterinarian is your dog's breeder. If you live near your breeder, you may even be able to use the same vet. Even if you don't live close by, though, your breeder will likely be able to point you in a good direction.

Your veterinarian will be one of the most important people in your Cocker's life—make sure that both you and your dog are comfortable with the vet you select.

Other great places to go for the names of trustworthy veterinarians in your area are your local animal shelter, breed clubs and rescue organizations, and even friends and family. When asking for a referral from a friend, ask the person not only *if* she would recommend a particular vet, but also *why*. Also, ask people if there is anything about their vets that they would change. You can usually distinguish the people who have stayed with their vets out of habit from those who feel passionate about their choices by asking this question.

Schedule a Tour

Once you have a starting point, schedule a tour of the facility. During this time, you should be able to meet the staff, including the veterinarians and technicians, and ask any questions you may have about the hospital's philosophies and policies. Asking to tour the hospital is a reasonable request and one that should be met with a welcoming response. Although you may be asked to wait until a typically slower part of the day or week (also very reasonable), beware of any hospital that resists showing you around its facilities.

HEALTH

Questions to Ask When Choosing a Vetrinarian

- Is the facility clean, comfortable, and well-organized?
- Are appointments required?
- How many veterinarians are in the practice?
- Are there technicians or other professional staff members?
- Are dogs and cats in separate areas?
- Is the staff caring, calm, competent, and courteous, and do they communicate effectively?
- Do the veterinarians have special interests, such as geriatrics or behavior?
- Do fees fit your budget, and are discounts for senior citizens or multi-pet households available?
- Are x-rays, ultrasound, blood work, EKG, endoscopy, and other diagnostics done in-house or referred to a specialist?
- Which emergency services are available?
- Is location and parking convenient?

(Courtesy of the Humane Society of the United States)

Location, Location, Location

Several factors may influence your decision. One of the most obvious is location. While more superficial details such as the appeal of the neighborhood and convenient parking may not be the best way to choose your dog's vet, where the office is located should legitimately make a difference in whether you select a particular vet. Distance, for example, can be an especially relevant issue if your dog ever needs immediate care. For this reason, you should try to find a veterinarian within a reasonable radius of your home.

Even if you find a veterinary hospital literally right around the corner from you, also look into the animal emergency clinics in your area. Most veterinary hospitals have specific hours of operation and refer clients to these special emergency facilities before or after their normal hours. You may also find that a vet who is 10 or 15 miles (16 or 24 kilometers) away is the best choice, and that is perfectly acceptable—providing that your English Cocker tolerates riding well and you have an alternate plan for emergencies.

153

Emergency hospitals have become an integral part of the veterinary community. When combined with the resources of conventional vet hospitals, these clinics specializing in crisis treatment offer pet owners the peace of mind of knowing that a vet is available 24 hours a day. If you are unsure whether your English Cocker's condition warrants emergency treatment, call ahead; a staff member should be able to advise you as to whether your dog should be seen immediately or if the problem can wait until the next day, when you can visit your regular veterinarian. Most owners seen by emergency vets are instructed to follow up with their regular vet at an appropriate time.

The Staff

Just as important as your veterinarian's location is the quality of the hospital's support staff. Whether you are simply phoning to schedule a routine examination or showing up unannounced because of an emergency, these are the first people you will deal with whenever your dog needs veterinary care. Are the employees friendly? Do they appear overworked or preoccupied? Are the veterinary technicians knowledgeable? How do they treat both the clients and their pets? If your vet shows good judgment in the selection of these people, it shows that client satisfaction is a priority. Capable people tend to surround themselves with other capable people. The same thing may be said about friendly ones.

You should feel as comfortable with your veterinarian as you do with her staff. Although your vet has considerably more knowledge and experience dealing with animals, as your dog's owner, you should be included in all decisions relating to your English Cocker Spaniel's care. One of your veterinarian's primary responsibilities is explaining all matters of your dog's treatment to you clearly and in language you can understand so that you can make the best possible decisions for your pet. If the vet talks down to you or doesn't take your questions seriously, keep looking for someone who does treat you with respect.

A minor personality conflict may be worth working through, but if you truly do not like a particular veterinarian, listen to your instincts. Anything that affects your ability to focus on the most important issue—your English Cocker's health—should be considered. Even if everything else about a hospital seems to be on the mark, a bad rapport with the vet can be a deal breaker.

Your Responsibilities

It is important to remember that your veterinarian isn't the only person with significant responsibilities. Your mutual goal is the well-being of your English Cocker Spaniel, an objective you wouldn't want your vet to take lightly—and one that you shouldn't either. You can help ensure that your vet can do the best job possible by keeping your dog in the best shape possible. This means feeding a nutritious diet, providing your pet with plenty of physical exercise and mental stimulation, and maintaining healthy grooming habits (such as regular teeth brushing). Good health begins at home.

You also owe it to your dog's vet to be a conscientious client. This means showing up for appointments on time, listening to what the vet has to say and answering questions about your dog's health before asking your own, and remembering to bring along any stool or urine samples that may have been requested when you made your appointment. Technically, veterinarians work for pet owners, but ideally the two should work together.

Of course, there is no need to look for a new vet if you already have one, unless you have been dissatisfied with the care your pets have received in the past. If this is the case, you owe it to your new English Cocker Spaniel to find a veterinarian with whom you will

When you first acquire your dog, research nearby veterinary hospitals and animal clinics to determine where you will take him in the event of an emergency.

both be comfortable. If you are lucky enough to already have such a vet, your only mission will be scheduling your new English Cocker Spaniel's first appointment.

PHYSICAL EXAMINATIONS

First Checkup

Schedule your English Cocker's first veterinary checkup as soon as you know when you will be bringing your new dog home. If you are buying a puppy from a pet store, it is especially important that you look over your health guarantee, as it will likely require that this exam be conducted within a few days of your purchase. If you are not working within these stringent guidelines, though, you may want to schedule the appointment in regards to your puppy's vaccination schedule, since your puppy will likely be due for shots relatively soon.

The Puppy Exam

Bringing along a stool sample is always a good idea, since your vet can rule out many internal parasites this way. Feed your English Cocker about an hour before you need to leave for the appointment; this should help produce an adequate specimen. Using a plastic sandwich bag, collect the stool. You can then drop the plastic bag into an opaque brown paper lunch sack for discreet transport. As long as collection is made within this time period, there is no need to refrigerate the specimen. If you prefer, you can collect the specimen the night before your dog's appointment and refrigerate it overnight. Never freeze a sample, though.

Once you arrive at the veterinary hospital, a technician will check and record your English Cocker Spaniel's weight and body temperature, along with your answers to a number of general questions pertaining to your dog's history and recent behavior. From whom did you get your English Cocker? What are you feeding your dog, and how has he been eating since arriving home? How has housetraining been going?

After looking over this information, your veterinarian will conduct a thorough physical examination, checking your English Cocker's eyes, ears, teeth, heart and lungs, joints and kneecaps, and coat and skin. Now is the time for you to ask any questions you may have relating to your dog's health. That teacher you had

During a physical exam, your vet will check your dog's eyes, ears, teeth, heart and lungs, joints and kneecaps, and coat and skin.

in ninth grade was right—there are no stupid questions—so don't be afraid of appearing uninformed for asking about something your vet might consider elementary. A big part of your vet's job is to educate her clients about basic animal care. I assure you there is hardly a question your veterinarian hasn't already heard.

Vaccination Schedule

Your breeder will have begun your English Cocker Spaniel's vaccination schedule before the dog is transferred to your care, but your puppy will likely be due for boosters (repeated doses of vaccines that ensure effectiveness) shortly after his homecoming. Bring all the paperwork you received from your breeder to your dog's first appointment so that your veterinarian knows what vaccines have already been administered. Between the rabies vaccine (which cannot be given until a pup is at least 12 weeks old) and boosters for distemper and parvovirus, you will be visiting your veterinarian frequently within the first few weeks. You will also need to decide if you wish for your English Cocker to be vaccinated against any optional afflictions, such as kennel cough and Lyme disease.

Bear in mind that while frequent trips to the veterinarian for your dog's initial vaccinations can be both costly and demanding of your time, the best thing you can do for your English Cocker Spaniel's health is spread out these inoculations. Some shots

Cold, Wet Noses Are Good, Right?

A cold, wet nose is one sign of good health in dogs and cats. However, even a healthy pet can have a warm, dry nose on occasion. On the other hand, really sick pets can also have cold, wet noses. What does all this mean? Simply that any one indicator of health is not 100 percent accurate all the time. Sick pets with cold noses should be seen by your veterinarian. And by the same token, pets with warm, dry noses who are showing other symptoms, such as lethargy or not eating, should also be seen by a doctor.

(Courtesy of the American Animal Hospital Association and Healthypet.com)

already contain several different vaccines. Increasing the number of shots your dog receives in one visit may also increase your English Cocker's chances of suffering from related problems. In mild cases, this may mean mild side effects such as minor pain, redness, and swelling. In more serious situations, side effects can include anaphylaxis (a severe allergic reaction), autoimmune hemolytic anemia (AIHA), and possibly even death.

Opinions differ somewhat as to the level of these risks, but most veterinarians would agree that limiting the vaccinations your dog receives during a given visit can only help reduce these risks. One Cocker breeder I know will only administer the distemper combo shot alone. She won't give it with anything else—not the Lyme or rabies vaccine, no heartworm or flea preventative, not even when a dog is in heat.

An Education in Vaccinations

Commonly made up of infinitesimal amounts of the viruses they aim to prevent, vaccines works by stimulating a dog's own natural immunities. When a vaccine is injected into your English Cocker's body, it is immediately recognized as a foreign agent. In response, antibodies are rapidly produced to combat this intruder, setting a vital precedent. If the same agent assaults your dog again, his body will respond even more quickly.

Some vaccines are required by boarding kennels, daycare programs, and other canine-centered businesses. Boosters may also need to be given annually, twice per year, or once every three years depending on the type of vaccine. *Nosodes*, homeopathic inoculations, may sometimes fulfill these requirements. Although the protocol varies from region to region, many veterinarians have recently lengthened their recommended timetables for many vaccines after reviewing research showing that immunity provided by many inoculations lasts far longer than initially thought. While periodic boosters are necessary, recent findings suggest that vaccinating too frequently may actually be compromising our dogs' immune systems and leaving them particularly vulnerable to other afflictions, such as acute allergies, epilepsy, and certain autoimmune diseases.

As with the related issue of how many vaccines are safe to administer at once, members of the veterinary community also have differing views about how often is too often for regular inoculations. The best precaution is keeping abreast of the latest research relating to the safety of all canine vaccinations and making decisions for your dog's care after discussing these issues with a veterinarian you trust. Whatever the problems with the past or current vaccination protocol, abstaining from vaccinating entirely is definitely *not* the answer. Vaccinations protect your dog from a number of debilitating conditions.

Annual Checkups

Once your dog has received all his vaccinations (usually between the ages of four and six months), he will be old enough

Talk to your vet about which vaccinations will be necessary for your English Cocker to receive.

to be spayed or neutered. After this all-important procedure, your English Cocker will then only need to be seen for routine veterinary care and treatment for the occasional illness or injury. If your vet is open to the idea, though, I highly recommend bringing your dog in to your veterinary hospital periodically throughout the year, so he can get to know the staff and learn that not every trip to the vet's office involves being poked with thermometers and needles. Receiving a tasty treat from a technician without an ulterior motive may likely ease your dog's stress a bit when the time comes for his next more formal visit.

If you prefer to spread out the cost of recurring care, you may spread your dog's visits over two or three appointments throughout the year. I bring my two Cockers in separately for their annual physicals (spaced several months apart) and then together when it's time for their heartworm tests and preventive medications in the spring. Some vets may require that you bring your dogs in at the same time to earn a multi-pet discount, so check into this before making your appointments.

Annual physical examinations make it much easier to catch potential health problems before they become more serious.

The Annual Exam

Your dog's annual checkups will be very similar to his first veterinary visit. Each year, your vet will examine your English Cocker from head to tail, looking for early signs of illnesses that may be treated or effectively avoided with early intervention. She will thoroughly check your dog's eyes, ears, nose, and mouth. Next, the heart and lungs will be examined for any congestion or other abnormalities. Reflexes will also be checked. The vet will inspect your English Cocker's coat and skin, searching for cuts and scrapes, fleas and ticks, and general dullness—an early sign of many serious illnesses.

No body part should be overlooked; your dog should be thoroughly checked for any suspicious lumps or bumps, as well as any enlarged internal organs. Your vet will feel your English Cocker's lymph nodes for symmetry, size, and tenderness. Your dog's genitals will also be checked for abnormal discharge, color, and swelling. While conducting these more literal parts of the exam, your vet will also be observing your dog's overall behavior, which is an important indicator of how your dog is feeling.

When the technician calls your dog's name, one of the first things she will do is weigh your English Cocker and take his temperature. At this time, you will likely be asked a few routine questions about your dog's recent health and behavior, as well as if you have any specific questions or concerns relating to your dog's care. Many times, your veterinary technician can readily address routine questions, but don't hesitate to follow up on any answers with your veterinarian. A good technician will record the key aspects of your conversation in your dog's chart for your vet to review with you during the exam. You will also be reminded of which vaccines your dog is due to receive and asked which ones you wish to have administered that day. Generally the technician will ready the vaccines, but the vet will actually give the shots.

Your English Cocker Spaniel's annual physical can be one of the most important precautions you take for his well being. Since your dog cannot use words to let you know when he is feeling poorly, this exam may provide you with vital information about a condition that would otherwise go unnoticed until it has progressed to a more serious stage. For this reason, you must never skip a routine appointment. Even if your dog appears to be in perfect health, remember that appearances are often deceiving—many serious illnesses begin with no outwards symptoms whatsoever. Dogs can be much more resilient than we are, so we have to take a proactive role in maintaining their good health.

Other Vaccinations

Other important vaccinations include distemper and parvovirus. These are most commonly given annually, but the recommended timetable for this combination shot may also be extended in the future.

SPAYING AND NEUTERING

When I was a little girl, I used to watch the game show "The Price Is Right" and listen to Bob Barker sign off every day urging his audience to "help control the pet population; have your pet spayed or neutered." My family believed in this cause deeply, so even then I knew what this meant. Today, I feel just as strongly about the significance of this very important part of pet ownership, but now I also know that there are even more reasons for spaying and neutering our animals.

Benefits

Spaying your female English Cocker Spaniel eliminates the risk

Don't Forget Your English Cocker's Eyes

Just as your English Cocker Spaniel must receive routine veterinary exams, his eyes also need regular checkups. Even if your English Cocker's eyes appear healthy, regular ophthalmological checkups will help ensure that they stay that way. Although vision loss may be unavoidable with some diseases, the early detection of others could save your dog's eyesight. Since eye problems are prevalent in English Cocker Spaniels, you owe it to your dog to keep an eye on his visual health.

If your regular veterinary office doesn't offer ophthalmological evaluation, your vet should be able to direct you to a qualified caregiver in your area. A dog should be at least 8 to 12 weeks old before having an eye exam, since the size of the eye in younger pups can make a proper examination difficult. If a congenital problem is found, be sure to notify your breeder. The owners of your dog's littermates should also be told so that they may bring their dogs to be checked, as well. English Cockers with healthy eyes should be seen for checkups approximately every three years, but once a problem has been detected, a dog should then be seen annually.

of ovarian and uterine cancers, as well as potentially deadly uterine infections, known as pyometra. It also significantly reduces the risk of breast cancer later in your dog's life. Neutering your male dog offers similar advantages, including the prevention of testicular cancer and lowered risks of prostate cancer, hernias, and bleeding anal tumors. By making this one simple decision, you can help your dog live a longer, healthier life.

Spaying involves the removal of a female dog's ovaries and uterus, making it impossible for the dog to become pregnant. Spayed females also no longer experience heat, the phase that immediately precedes ovulation in dogs—a time that can be quite frustrating for owners, since it involves messy vaginal bleeding and the much-unwanted attention of interested male dogs. Neutering, the equivalent procedure for males, entails the removal of the testicles; this in turn removes the dog's ability to impregnate a female. The neutering process also usually lessens the number of annoying behaviors displayed by the dog—issues such as marking or even aggression.

For all their advantages, both spaying and neutering are very straightforward surgical procedures; neither poses significant risk to the dog. Unless you plan on breeding or showing your dog, you should have your English Cocker Spaniel sterilized by the time he or she is six months old. A show dog should be "fixed" (the laymen's term for this kind of operation) as soon as he has finished his confirmation activities; a breeding dog should be sterilized when he or she will no longer be utilized for breeding.

Not Every Dog Should be Bred

Although we all may imagine from time to time that our pets might make ideal parents or produce glorious offspring, it is essential to understand that very few English Cocker Spaniels actually possess the long list of traits that are crucial for ideal breeding. Responsible breeders make great efforts to ensure that a dog is a prime candidate for breeding before ever taking any steps in that direction. They carefully inspect every nuance of both appearance and temperament, they test for dangerous conditions common to the breed, and they seek the opinions of other experienced English Cocker Spaniel authorities. Often this is accomplished by showing the animal repeatedly in conformation

Spaying or neutering your dog offers numerous benefits, including reduced likelihood of cancer and other illnesses.

events prior to making a final decision. They also demand the same standards from any dog they select as a potential mate for theirs.

Even when these precautions are taken, an experienced breeder can still produce a puppy that suffers from any number of medical problems. It isn't uncommon for one or more puppies to be stillborn, or to require euthanasia due to a devastating and irreversible condition. Every breeder I know has told me that losing puppies this way is one of the worst parts of the breeding process. These are the risks, under even the best conditions. Since most owners have so little experience with dog breeding, it is best to let any musings about breeding our pets stay in the theoretical realm and to leave the awesome responsibility of breeding English Cocker Spaniels to those who are up to the task.

Finally, no one can overlook the gargantuan problem of animal overpopulation, and the obvious benefits that spaying and neutering offer in helping to reduce the number of unwanted dogs in shelters—a number that is currently in the range of six to eight million in the US alone. As compassionate dog owners, we *all* have responsibility in controlling the pet population.

ENGLISH COCKER SPANIEL HEALTH ISSUES

There isn't a single dog breed that is not prone to at least a few specific diseases or genetic abnormalities. Although some breeds are certainly susceptible to more problems than others, no breed is entirely free of these kinds of issues. Be very leery of any breeder who tries to tell you otherwise.

Fortunately, most English Cocker–specific conditions are manageable, but good breeders take reasonable steps to help lower the risk of many of these afflictions in their litters. Healthy parents usually produce healthy offspring, but what exactly determines a healthy animal? Breeders not only have an obligation to remove afflicted dogs from their breeding programs, but they also have a responsibility to predict conditions that may likely beset certain dogs in the future and refrain from breeding those animals, as well. Genetic testing and certified evaluations are valuable resources in the breeding process for this reason.

Generally, the most common tests performed on English Cocker Spaniels are to clear potential parents for eye and hip problems. For example, you may frequently hear from an English Cocker breeder that a particular dog has been certified through the Kennel Club/BVA Hip Scoring scheme; this means that the Kennel Club (KC) and the British Veterinary Association (BVA) have tested this English Cocker Spaniel to confirm normal hip confirmation. A similar scheme is available for screening dogs for common eye conditions, such as progressive retinal atrophy (PRA).

Even the healthiest parents, though, can produce a puppy that will go on to experience one or more health problems as an adult. Senior dogs are at a particular risk of many illnesses common in numerous breeds. Your dog may never be confronted with any of the following conditions, but arming yourself with information about them will enable you to help your dog through whatever lies ahead.

Autoimmune Diseases

Autoimmune diseases are unique in that they cause a dog's own immune system to turn on itself. In the case of autoimmune hemolytic anemia (AIHA), the dog's red blood cells are attacked, robbing the body of their oxygen-carrying properties. Once destroyed, these cells are then passed through the dog's body as urine. Sometimes the cause of AIHA can be identified, such as with AIHA secondary to systemic lupus erythematosus (SLE). More often, however, the source cannot be verified. In many of these cases, the cause is often theorized to be a bacterial infection, medication, or vaccination.

Although the disease is treatable, battling AIHA can be difficult. Steroids are usually the preferred treatment option, but if the condition does not improve with their use alone, blood transfusions and chemotherapy may also be necessary. Symptoms of AIHA include discolored urine (from expelled blood), pale complexion, and fatigue. A dog with AIHA may also have jaundice, a condition that presents with a yellow discoloration of the eyes, nose, and skin. As blood is lost, the dog's body weakens rapidly, so early diagnosis is vital.

Autoimmune thyroiditis is similar

to AIHA, but instead of targeting red blood cells, autoimmune thyroiditis causes a dog's immune system to attack its own T_3 and T_4 thyroid hormones. The condition also destroys thyroglobulin, a substance necessary for forming such hormones. The symptoms of autoimmune thyroiditis are very similar to those of hypothyroidism, since the same system is being compromised in both situations. Diagnosis and treatment are also similar, but in the case of autoimmune thyroiditis, thyroid antibodies will be found in the dog's blood when tested.

Deafness

Although not as prominent in English Cocker Spaniels as in many other breeds, congenital deafness does occur in English Cockers, primarily those with white pigmentation and blue eyes. The actual hearing loss typically takes place in the first few weeks after birth due to the degeneration of blood supply to the inner ear, or cochlea. In response to this, the nerve cells of the cochlea die, and permanent deafness results. This may affect one or both ears.

You may be wondering if ear infections can ultimately lead to hearing loss. The answer is a qualified yes. If a dog suffers from recurrent ear infections—even mild ones—deafness may occur, but permanent deafness might still be avoidable with proper treatment.

Reputable breeders make every effort to prevent genetic illnesses from infiltrating their dogs.

There are also several other possible causes for canine deafness, including toxicities, injuries, and the natural aging process. These losses may be full or partial, but are usually permanent.

If your English Cocker loses his hearing, a few precautions should help keep your dog and other household members safe. First, since deaf animals tend to startle more easily than hearing ones, people within the household (particularly children) should be warned against startling the dog. It is also especially important that

Inherited Conditions

Are there any inherited conditions of which I should be aware?

Yes. Although the best breeders make every effort to avoid breeding from stock genetically carrying conditions that are known sometimes to affect dogs, these are not always easy to detect. Progressive retinal atrophy (PRA; night blindness), which may not be detected until the dog is 5 years old or more, and familial nephropathy (a fatal type of kidney failure that affects young dogs up to about 18 months of age) are the main conditions that have been identified and are being eradicated by careful selection of breeding stock. The KC and the BVA run schemes under which committed breeders can have their breeding stock examined and tested for PRA and also hip dysplasia (a condition that may affect the hip joint of dogs). Good breeders only breed from stock over 18 months of age and screened under one or more of the schemes. These schemes are voluntary, not compulsory. Work is currently being done on identifying problems by DNA and a gene test for prcd_PRA, the gene involved in PRA, is now available via the American company, Optigen. More information can be found at www.thecockerspanielclub.co.uk/health.htm.

(Courtesy of The Cocker Spaniel Club)

a deaf dog not be allowed to walk off leash when outdoors, since he cannot hear the auditory warning signs of impending dangers, such as cars or other animals.

Most dogs can still function very well with a hearing disability. Some changes will obviously need to be made in your training program, such as the use of hand signals in lieu of verbal commands, but most English Cockers cope surprisingly well with the loss of this seemingly essential canine sense.

Ear Infections

The English Cocker Spaniel's pendulous ears leave the breed particularly vulnerable to ear infections. With the ear leather lying so closely against the ear canal, airflow is severely restricted; this results in trapped moisture—a breeding ground for infection. Although usually caused by bacteria or yeast, ear infections known as *otitis externa* can also result from wax build-up, an overabundance of hair inside the ear, or a foreign body that has become lodged in the ear canal. They can also be secondary to other kinds of bodily infections. When *otitis externa* spreads to the middle ear, the result is *otitis media*, a more serious infection. A ruptured eardrum can also cause *otitis media*.

Interestingly, the conventional English Cocker haircut, which includes clipping the face and upper third of the ear short, actually helps prevent ear infections from occurring by maximizing airflow. Factors that may contribute to an English Cocker's predisposition to ear infections include insufficient drying after bathing or swimming and using too much ear cleanser or harsh products when cleaning the ears. A naturally narrow ear canal can also place a dog at greater risk.

If your English Cocker Spaniel is suffering from either type of ear infection, it will be hard to miss the signs. Your dog will likely shake his head or scratch at his ears uncontrollably in response to the discomfort. Tilting of the head in one direction is also a sign of an ear infection. The ear itself may appear red or swollen, with or without a black or yellowish discharge. Often, a strong, offensive odor also emanates from the infected ear.

Did You Know?

AIHA tends to strike females more often than males, but autoimmune thyroiditis appears to affect both genders equally.

At the first sign of an ear infection, bring your dog to a veterinarian for an examination. The vet will need to make sure the eardrum is not ruptured before prescribing a medication, as some drugs can lead to hearing loss if this is the case.

As tempting as it may be to clean the ear before bringing your English Cocker to be examined, you will be doing both your dog and your vet a favor by abstaining from doing so. Even a mild cleanser will likely irritate your English Cocker's already sore ear once it is infected, so for now this task is best left for the professionals. Also, being able to look at the ear through an otoscope will help your vet diagnose the problem. She may also wish to take a sample from the ear canal for inspection under a microscope.

Once a diagnosis has been made, your vet will probably prescribe an antibiotic to clear up the infection. A middle ear infection can take up to several weeks to resolve completely, but most cases of otitis externa improve relatively quickly once treatment has begun. An ear infection is not a problem that will go away on its own; veterinary treatment must be sought. With proper treatment and sensible precautions taken in the future, however, ear infections don't have to be a recurrent problem.

Epilepsy

A good friend of mine once telephoned me in tears, frantically describing an incident that had just occurred with her two-year-old American Cocker Spaniel. She said that the problem had apparently passed, but that just moments before the call her dog had seemed to lose all awareness of her surroundings, moving her head slowly back and forth with an odd, glazed look upon her face. She had thought her dog was in the process of dying until she suddenly came out of this odd trance just as quickly as she had slipped into it. I knew instantly what had happened, for the same thing had happened several times to my parents' then four-year-old Cocker. My friend's dog had suffered a minor seizure.

Most frequently the result of a condition called idiopathic epilepsy (the word *idiopathic* meaning the cause is not known), canine seizures can be frightening for both dogs and owners. A seizing dog may shake uncontrollably, staring into space (typically signs of a petit mal seizure) or fall to his side, drool, and make a paddling motion with his legs (signs of a grand mal seizure)—all for no apparent reason. Sometimes after the seizure, the dog may pant heavily and relieve himself with little or no notice.

There are many old wives' tales about seizures, including the notion that an animal can swallow his tongue during the episode; rest assured this is *not* the case. Putting your fingers in the mouth of a seizing animal can, however, be dangerous for you, as even the most amiable dog may bite when in the midst of the experience. Making sure your dog does not harm himself (by bumping into anything, for instance) during a seizure is a good idea, but keep your hands and face away from his mouth at all times.

Deafness is not especially common in English Cockers, but they are prone to ear infections, which can lead to hearing problems over time.

The most important thing to remember if your dog ever experiences a seizure is probably one of the most difficult—remain calm. Doing so will help you best observe what is happening so that you can relay this information to your veterinarian. If the seizure passes within a few minutes, you can wait to contact your vet until it has passed. If it continues longer than this, however, you should bring your dog to the veterinary hospital immediately.

Since seizures can sometimes be a sign of other illnesses, such as liver disease, kidney disease, and cancer, your dog should be examined to help rule out these conditions. Your vet may suggest running a blood profile for this reason. Idiopathic epilepsy is usually the reason for seizures in dogs less than five years of age, but older dogs are at a higher risk for problems that might be the culprit, such as a tumor in the central nervous system.

If your dog has suffered one or more idiopathic seizures, you may wish to start keeping a journal of the incidences. Record the date and time, the length of the seizure, a detailed description of what happens during the episode, and also a brief account of what happens before and after the seizure. This information could be especially helpful to your vet in regards to your English Cocker's treatment plan.

It is no coincidence that both my mother's Cocker and my friend's dog both experienced this unpleasant experience. Cocker Spaniels—both American and English—are prone to epilepsy, but fortunately the condition is usually highly manageable. In many cases of idiopathic epilepsy, treatment isn't even necessary. However, if your dog is experiencing seizures more often than once a month, or if the episodes are lasting several minutes each, your vet may suggest placing your dog on an oral anticonvulsant medication. The most common of these is phenobarbital.

Eye Problems

"They have a lot of eye problems, don't they?" If you own an English Cocker Spaniel, you have likely been asked this highly rhetorical question at least once. It is indeed widely known that English Cockers are one of several breeds most commonly diagnosed with ocular diseases.

Cataracts

Although prevalent, cataracts are fortunately painless and also highly treatable. The word cataract literally means *to break down*; in the case of this ophthalmological condition, it is the transparency of the eye's lens that essentially breaks down, leaving an opaque film over the dog's eye. This film (or cataract), which interrupts the dog's vision, is usually extremely noticeable to an observant owner. Cataracts may be inherited or caused by a traumatic injury to the dog's eye. (The latter type will only affect the eye that has been wounded.)

Although there is no way to prevent or reverse cataracts, they can be surgically removed and replaced with an acrylic lens by a veterinary ophthalmologist. This procedure offers an impressive success rate of 90 to 95 percent in otherwise healthy dogs.

Help for Deaf Dogs

For ideas on how to best acclimate your hearing-impaired English Cocker to the world around him, and to learn new ways of communicating with your pet, read *Living with a Deaf Dog: A Book of Advice, Facts, and Experiences About Canine Deafness* by Susan C. Becker.

Interestingly, this statistic remains the same regardless of how long a dog has had cataracts.

A third cause of cataracts can be the onset of diabetes. In this unique situation, the progression of the cataracts may actually be decelerated with successful treatment of the diabetes.

Cherry Eye

This affliction, formally known as nictitans gland prolapse (NGP), affects a dog's third eyelid. If you did not realize that your English Cocker even had a third eyelid, you are not alone. Many owners learn of this additional lower lid only when the tear gland behind it becomes red and inflamed, protruding from the corner of the dog's eye. If left untreated, the mass may become infected due to prolonged exposure. Your English Cocker may also scratch at the eye, compounding the problem.

Although the exact cause of this condition is unknown, it is believed to be the result of a weakness of the ligament that holds the nictitans gland in place, which causes the gland to move out of its normal position spontaneously.

Cherry eye is usually not painful to the dog, but it can be quite alarming to an unsuspecting owner upon discovery. In mild cases, a veterinarian will prescribe a steroid to reduce the swelling, but positive results are often only temporary. Since long-term steroid use is usually best avoided, surgery is frequently the ideal solution.

Surgery for cherry eye once included the removal of the tear gland, but fewer vets are taking this approach, as eliminating the gland leaves a dog more vulnerable to keratoconjunctivitis sicca (KCS), or dry eye. KCS is a serious condition that can result in redness, mucus discharge, corneal scarring and ulceration, and ultimately even permanent sight loss.

Glaucoma

You may often hear the word "glaucoma" mentioned together with cataracts, but these are in fact two very different diseases. Unlike cataracts, which technically don't require treatment, glaucoma is a very serious disease that demands immediate medical attention. Also unlike cataracts, glaucoma can be very painful.

Caused by intraocular pressure (pressure within the dog's eyeball), glaucoma may present with redness, cloudiness, tearing, loss of vision, an enlarged eyeball, uncharacteristic aggressiveness, lethargy, or a loss of appetite. The disease is most often congenital, but in rare cases, it can be caused by a coexisting condition—a luxating (floating) cataract that blocks the natural fluid drainage of the dog's eye. Regardless of its cause, glaucoma can result in irreversible vision loss within mere hours if the pressure is not relieved.

Progressive Retinal Atrophy and Progressive Retinal Degeneration

Unfortunately, not all diseases that cause canine blindness can be alleviated with early intervention or surgical procedures. PRA and progressive retinal degeneration (PRD) are two inherited disorders that cause gradual but inevitable vision loss. This is caused by the deterioration or atrophy (shrinkage) of the retina. An English Cocker with PRA or PRD will likely begin bumping into things at night or in low-light situations, but will eventually show signs of increasing vision loss regardless of the time of day or light quality. Although PRA and PRD have further symptoms (including dilated pupils and hyperreflectivity, or shininess, to the back of the eye), these signs are rarely noticeable until the disease has already reached an advanced stage.

If every cloud indeed has a silver lining, for PRA and PRD it is the amount of time that an owner is given to help prepare for her dog's eventual sight loss. Although it is natural for an owner to feel overwhelmed at first by the prognosis of permanent blindness, it is important to realize that your English Cocker Spaniel will be impacted by this deficit far less than a human being in a similar situation. Blind dogs can live enormously satisfying lives. Although some additional training will be necessary, most sightless English Cockers acclimate to this change easily by simply doing what they have always done—relying on their other, more valued senses, particularly hearing and smell.

If your dog is faced with any of these ocular conditions, give yourself some time to accept this unexpected turn of events, but know that the ordeal won't be nearly as dreadful as you might fear. After an initial adjustment period, both you and your dog will be able to enjoy a surprisingly normal life together, despite your English Cocker's visual impairment.

Food Allergies

My dogs' breeder shared with me recently that she suspects food allergies to be more common in Cocker Spaniels than other breeds. I, too, had wondered about this. It is estimated that 20 percent of dogs in the US suffer from some type of allergy, but my first American Cocker Spaniel seemed to have more food-related allergies than all of my friends' various dogs combined. Potatoes, tomatoes, and corn seemed to top Jonathan's list. For my breeders' dogs, the main culprit was chicken. While many veterinarians insist that the risk of food allergies is consistent among all dog breeds, some clinical findings suggest that English Cockers (along with several other breeds) are indeed predisposed to this problem.

The most common symptom of a canine food allergy is severe itching. A dog may react by incessantly scratching, biting, licking, or rubbing the itchy area—often to the point of inflicting self-trauma. Although rare, a dog may also show gastrointestinal signs of an allergy to a particular food. My Johnny would inevitably vomit every time a guest would unknowingly aggravate the situation by sharing a potato chip or small piece of pizza with him. (At one point, I actually considered hanging a sign in my kitchen reading *Please Don't Feed the Dog!*".) Other dogs may suffer from diarrhea as an effect of the offending food. In some instances, there may be a discharge from the eyes or nose; an affected dog may even cough or sneeze. Seizures and asthmatic reactions have also been reported as symptoms of severe canine food allergies.

Because food allergies can develop over time, your dog may suddenly experience an adverse reaction to a food or ingredient that has never been an issue in the past. (When Jonathan was a puppy, I invariably gave him my last potato chip whenever I indulged in the salty treat, and at the time he showed no intolerance to the snack whatsoever.) This kind of unprecedented reaction can make identifying the cause of your dog's allergy difficult, but not impossible.

If you or your vet suspect that your English Cocker is suffering from a food allergy, placing your dog on a hypoallergenic diet can help determine the cause (or causes) of the reaction. These specialized (or prescription) diets are frequently available only through veterinarians. Common canine food allergens include corn, beef, dairy products, wheat, and soybeans. Although allergy tests are available, they can be relatively expensive and not

Alternative Treatments for Seizures

Some complementary forms of medicine have also been found to help reduce the frequency and duration of seizures. One German shepherd owner I know has found qi gong (pronounced chi-KUNG) to be enormously helpful. This ancient Chinese healing technique focuses on exercise and mediation. Acupuncture, another complementary treatment, is also frequently used to help manage the condition.

Help for Blind Dogs

If you are noticing signs of vision loss in your English Cocker Spaniel, talk to your veterinarian about scheduling an ophthalmological exam. You can also contact the American College of Veterinary Ophthalmologists (ACVO) at www.acvo.com for a referral. If blindness is imminent, or even if your dog has already lost his sight, there is a wonderful book available called *Living with Blind Dogs*. Written by Caroline Levin, RN, this informative guide offers practical advice on how owners can best deal with sight loss in their pets.

always accurate. Once your dog has demonstrated a tolerance for the specialized diet (usually after at least several weeks), new ingredients may be added back into your dog's feeding regimen, one at a time so that you can tell which foods are the likeliest causes of the allergic reactions. Owners must be patient through this challenging process, which can take up to several months.

Most importantly, don't let an apparent allergy go untreated. Dogs do not understand that persistent scratching can cause secondary issues, such as infections; they will simply react to itching by scratching in one form or another every time. Medicated shampoos and conditioners and topical creams, ointments, or sprays may offer some relief. Whenever possible, avoiding the allergen altogether is best. Bringing your dog to the vet at the first sign of an allergy can place your dog on the road to identification before a serious secondary problem is triggered.

Hemophilia

A hereditary disease that causes a deficiency in blood clotting, hemophilia affects certain lines of English Cocker Spaniels. Carried by the females (through the X chromosome), the disease most commonly affects male dogs, although some females have been known to suffer from hemophilia when close inbreeding has taken place. The condition may present itself as early as puppyhood; persistent bleeding may occur when tails are docked, when dewclaws are removed, or when primary teeth begin to erupt through the dog's gums. It can also cause lameness when bleeding occurs into muscles or joints after a routine vaccination. Although rare, death can occur suddenly and at any time if bleeding occurs into the brain or spinal cord.

Not all dogs who suffer from hemophilia show early symptoms. English Cockers with a mild form of the disease might not show any symptoms unless surgery or trauma results in excessive bleeding. Dogs showing overt symptoms of hemophilia (excessive bleeding termed "hemorrhaging") require immediate treatment by way of a blood transfusion with fresh or frozen plasma.

Owners of hemophiliac canines must be constantly vigilant of their dogs' environment, minimizing risks of bleeding wherever possible. Ideally, all furniture within the home should be cushioned, and any sharp corners or edges should be affixed with childproofing guards. Some veterinarians recommend feeding only soft foods, and no bones whatsoever. Even if severe bleeding is avoided, however, periodic blood transfusions may still be required. A strict resting period after a transfusion is essential to prevent hemorrhaging. There is no cure for hemophilia.

If your English Cocker is diagnosed with this disorder, it is especially important that you inform the breeder so she can have your dog's parents tested. The dam (the mother of the litter) is almost certainly the carrier. Ideally, an English Cocker affected with hemophilia should be kept as an only pet so that bites and scratches from other animals will be less likely.

Hip Dysplasia

When many of us hear the term "hip dysplasia", we immediately think of larger breeds such as German Shepherds and Labrador Retrievers, but surprisingly this problem is also quite common in smaller breeds like the English Cocker Spaniel. Although good breeders test for hip dysplasia, it can still occasionally appear in some dogs who have been cleared; there is no way to guarantee that a dog won't develop the condition.

Literally a malformation of the ball and socket in the hip joint, hip dysplasia is an inherited defect that usually doesn't develop until a dog is between six to eight months old. Although the condition may be mild, moderate, or severe, the signs are usually

English Cockers have a predisposition toward food allergies, so monitor your dog carefully to make sure he isn't experiencing problems with his diet.

Ideally, an English Cocker Spaniel affected with hemophilia should be kept as an only pet, so bites and scratches from other animals will be less likely to occur.

the same and include lameness, stiffness, and limping. Symptoms may be particularly intense on cold, damp days. A dog suffering from hip dysplasia may also exhibit an understandable change in temperament.

As the dog continues, however reluctantly, to move through the pain, the problem may seem to dissipate, but more likely this is simply the result of scar tissue that forms from the stretching and tearing of the joint. Eventually, arthritis also sets in and compounds the problem when symptoms return.

Diagnosis is made through veterinary examination and x-rays. A veterinarian may recommend surgery in extreme cases, but medical treatment is also possible. This may include enforced rest periods during times of acute discomfort, mild analgesics (pain killers), and anti-inflammatory drugs. Although surgical treatment may seem like a risky endeavor, many dogs return to a full activity level even after having a full hip replacement.

Hypothyroidism

Like people, dogs have two small, butterfly-shaped lobes situated behind the throat called the thyroid gland. While this gland is responsible for a number of functions within the body, its primary task is controlling your English Cocker's metabolism—the rate at which your dog processes his daily caloric intake from food. Hypothyroidism is a condition in which the thyroid gland becomes underactive, therefore leaving the affected dog particularly vulnerable to weight gain, loss of energy, and many other unpleasant side effects. A dog suffering from hypothyroidism may also experience skin problems, chronic ear infections, and even depression.

Weight gain is often the most blatant symptom of this condition, so inform your veterinarian if your English Cocker's weight suddenly increases without an apparent explanation, such as a more voracious appetite. If your vet suspects hypothyroidism, one or more blood tests will be administered to confirm the diagnosis. It is important to note that a number of different testing methods are available for diagnosing this condition, each with its own level of accuracy. Usually, more than one type of test is necessary for a reliable diagnosis. Although the differences between the tests may seem complex, your vet can explain the basic principles of each so that you can make an informed decision.

Once diagnosed, hypothyroidism may be treated with a daily dose of a synthetic thyroid hormone called thyroxine (levothyroxine). Although periodic checkups will be necessary to ensure proper dosing, most dogs with hypothyroidism remain symptom-free for the rest of their lives.

Luxating Patella

Like many other breeds, English Cocker Spaniels are susceptible to a number of knee problems, including patellar luxation. This condition, aggravated by excess weight, involves the dislocation of a small, flat bone at the front of the dog's hind knee. This loose kneecap can slip out of place either occasionally or frequently, making it difficult for the dog to place any weight on the affected leg. If you see your dog hopping around on just three legs, a luxating patella (sometimes referred to as slipped stifles) might be the problem.

Once your veterinarian has confirmed this diagnosis, she may suggest the use of an anti-inflammatory drug. If the problem persists, however, surgery may be necessary. As with other skeletal problems, arthritis may also develop as a result of this condition.

The exact cause of patellar luxation has not been determined, but it is particularly common in small breeds and is typically the result of a congenital or developmental problem. The condition is typically diagnosed early in a dog's life—within the first six months or so. Patellar luxation can also sometimes be caused (and definitely intensified) by the impact from falls, so it is particularly important that you not allow your English Cocker to jump from high places. This includes furniture situated high off the floor and stairs. Younger dogs, whose bodies are still growing, are especially susceptible to this kind of injury, so keep an even closer eye on those puppies.

Ruptured Cruciate Ligament

The anterior cruciate ligament (ACL) is a vulnerable part of a spaniel's body. A dog with a ruptured ACL will abstain from resting its weight on the injured leg—the first sign of the problem. Another sign is an extended rear leg when the dog is sitting. If the meniscus (a cartilage disk within the knee) has been torn, a popping sound may be heard when he walks. There may also be pain and swelling at the joint. Although the lameness may subside

Hip dysplasia is a common problem among English Cocker Spaniels, but can be treated through rest, medication, and possibly surgery.

after a while, it is very likely that it will return, because movement only causes further damage to this problem.

Although acupuncture worked well for my dog, it isn't necessarily the better choice for all English Cockers with this problem. Selecting a treatment plan for any affliction is a decision you should make together with your veterinarian, based on the individual details of your dog's situation. Friends of mine who also own Cockers have encountered this injury with one of their dogs, as well. They chose the route of surgery, and enjoyed the same level of success as I did with my Cocker. It is important to note that if the affected knee is left untreated, the greater the effects of arthritis will be when it sets in *and* the less effective surgery may be once it is performed.

Skin Problems

Although some skin problems are secondary to other issues (such as food allergies), English Cocker Spaniels have a predisposition to a skin condition called "primary seborrhea". Caused by an overproduction of skin cells, including sebaceous (oil) cells, the skin of dogs suffering from this problem becomes greasy and scaly. A foul odor may also be present. Eventually, lesions form, most commonly on the elbows, hocks, and ears. The skin may or may not itch.

Primary seborrhea is considered a chronic condition. Although no cure is available, treatment with medicated shampoos, ointments, antibiotics, or corticosteroids can be helpful in managing the condition.

DEALING WITH PARASITES

For many dog owners, just thinking about fleas and ticks is enough to prompt scratching. Our English Cocker Spaniels, though, have to deal with a bit more than itchy discomfort when confronted by these dangerous pests. These creatures have an uncanny knack for seeking out our precious pets and exposing them to a number of serious parasitic diseases. Fortunately, these illnesses are easily avoidable using simple preventive medications sold at most veterinary hospitals and also by a variety of new pet pharmacies that offer impressively competitive prices.

You might need to visit your dog's veterinarian before ordering preventive medication from a pet pharmacy, as a prescription may be necessary. Generally, this process is a simple one. Many companies will even contact your vet on your behalf before dispensing the medications.

Fleas

To some owners, fleas may seem like a fact of canine life—one that, in comparison to other parasitic pests, is more an annoyance than a danger—but the fact is these bothersome creatures can cause serious illness. Most dogs are allergic to the flea saliva left behind on their skin after the biting begins, and many will react automatically by scratching to the point of creating sores and skin infection. If left untreated, flea infestation can lead to anemia and even the transmission of tapeworms. For puppies and elderly pets, these effects can be disastrous, even deadly.

Although wingless, fleas are capable of jumping distances of 13 inches (33 cm) or farther horizontally, making it possible for them to spread from one animal to another with great efficiency. They also reproduce at an astounding rate, leaving entire households vulnerable to the havoc they wreak.

Fleas can be difficult to locate even on dogs with much shorter coats; on an English Cocker Spaniel they can be virtually

Cara the Cocker

English Cockers sometimes suffer from spinal deformities, also. These can in turn result in hip problems, as was the case with a Cocker named Cara, who belonged to a breeder friend of mine. Cara was born with an extra half vertebra that caused one hip to be misaligned. (Not all spinal deformities are serious or cause secondary problems.) My friend decided to spay her puppy and place her as a pet with a loving family instead of using her in her breeding program, as originally planned. Thankfully, however, the dog never experienced any issues relating to the misaligned hip. Cara is now eight years old and enjoying a very normal life with her new family in New England.

impossible to pinpoint, but persistent scratching is usually a reliable indicator of their presence. They usually target specific areas on a dog, including near the ears, on the neck and abdomen, and around the base of the tail.

Prevention and Treatment

Just like heartworm disease, the problem of fleas is easy to avoid, but the method of prevention you choose can drastically affect both the outcome and your dog's health. The safest and most effective route for combating fleas is to use preventive treatments recommended by your veterinarian. Some brands even prevent both fleas and heartworm disease with just a single medication. The majority of these treatments are applied topically to a small section of your dog's skin once a month. Once applied, the solution is absorbed through the skin and spreads, eliminating any fleas presently hiding within your dog's coat and preventing future infestation.

If your English Cocker Spaniel has fleas, you will need to take several important steps to eliminate the problem for good. First, see your veterinarian at once. In addition to treating your dog, you will also need to treat your dog's environment, which may span from the inside of your home to your back yard. Your vet's input can be invaluable in selecting the best plan of attack.

Younger dogs are prone to injuries that can aggravate patellar luxation, such as those sustained by falling or jumping from high places.

Because fleas thrive in warm temperatures, your home is an ideal haven for these long-lasting pests—even in the middle of winter. Carpets, furniture, and draperies all provide excellent refuge for fleas. Your house may be the cleanest on the block, but it won't make a bit of difference; the fleas will still make themselves right at home. They will also feast on any available target—your dog, your cat, even your children.

Because the most effective flea bombs (or foggers) are highly toxic, it is imperative that you read and follow all instructions very carefully. It is particularly important that you remove all people and pets from your home before treating it. If your home contains carpeting, remember to vacuum thoroughly after treatment is completed, and don't forget to throw away the bag immediately, whether it is full or not. It only takes a single flea to start a second wave of infestation.

Be sure to check with your veterinarian before using any over-the-counter flea or tick product. Organophosphate insecticides (OPs) and carbamates are found in various products and should be avoided, since they pose particular health threats to children and pets, even when used correctly. A product contains an OP if the ingredient list contains chlorpyrifos, dichlorvos, phosmet, naled, tetrachlorvinphos, diazinon, or malathion. The product contains a carbamate if the ingredient list includes carbaryl or propoxur.

Natural Alternatives

Natural products that are gentler for treating both pets and their environments are available. For example, herbal flea collars, sprays, and shampoos can be purchased as an alternative to ones containing pesticides. These products will repel fleas rather than kill them, so it is important to also use flea-trapping devices when going this route. Natural products sometimes also contain ingredients known for strengthening the canine immune system, since unhealthy dogs are especially prone to fleas and other parasites.

Heartworm

In the US, the heartworm is perhaps the best known of all canine parasites. In Europe, however, the risk for heartworm disease is substantially lower—with the exception of southern Europe, where the disease is much more prevalent. If you will be traveling with your English Cocker Spaniel, check with your veterinarian before embarking on your trip, particularly if your destinations include southern France, Spain, Italy, and other areas around the Mediterranean. She may prescribe heartworm preventive medication.

Heartworm disease passes from dog to dog by way of mosquito bites. Even dogs living in colder climates are at risk for this deadly disease. Since mosquitoes can exist in temperatures as low as 57°F (14°C), this means there are virtually no safe havens. A handful of

ACL Injuries and Acupuncture

My Cocker Jonathan suffered an injury to his ACL during a routine trip outdoors to relieve himself one January morning. He slipped on a patch of ice and started limping immediately. I assumed it was just a sprain, but for us, this small mishap marked the beginning of a six-month ordeal.

When I brought Johnny to the emergency vet, I was told that surgery would be virtually unavoidable, and that it would involve a painstaking three-month recovery. I was committed to doing whatever my dog needed, but I hated to resort to an invasive procedure unless there was no other option. Fortunately, my personal veterinarian thought that acupuncture would be worth trying first. We began with three visits a week, lasting about 20 minutes each. By the third visit, Johnny was showing improvement. We slowly lessened the frequency of his visits — down to one visit a week, then one visit every other week, etc. By July, his therapy was discontinued entirely, and he was essentially back to his old self once again. My vet did warn me, however, that once a dog suffers a ruptured ACL, the chances of experiencing the same injury to the other knee increase significantly — some statistics suggest an 80 percent chance within just one year.

cases are reported each year in Britain. The only sure-fire way of preventing the disease is to use monthly (or daily) preventatives year round. When used correctly, these protective treatments are approximately 100 percent effective. As an added advantage, heartworm preventive eliminates other intestinal parasites that may be in your dog's system, such as hookworms and roundworms.

Since dogs recently or lightly infected with heartworms may show no signs of the disease, it is important to have your dog's blood tested annually if you live in a warmer climate, preferably in the spring. Even if your dog is on a year-round preventive regimen, your English Cocker may become infected after just a single missed dose. Once a dog begins to show symptoms, they are likely to be severe, including coughing, exercise intolerance, and respiratory distress.

As the name implies, this disease targets a dog's heart, but the initial damage actually occurs in the lungs, where the heartworm infiltrates the animal's blood vessels, causing them to swell and become scarred. As blood flow becomes more and more restricted, blood pressure rises, resulting in hypertension. Without intervention, heart failure eventually ensues.

If your dog is diagnosed with heartworm disease, the prognosis will depend on how far the disease has progressed and whether any secondary conditions, such as liver or kidney problems, exist. At one time, treatment itself was a dangerous undertaking, but new medications have made treating even dogs with severe infestations considerably safer. Still, prevention is highly preferable

Dirty Puppy Disease

When a dog suffers from primary seborrhea, the excessive amount of oil in the skin traps dirt and other debris. Because of this, primary seborrhea is sometimes called "dirty puppy disease."

to treatment. Although treatment is now indeed less dangerous, it remains a complicated and expensive procedure.

Worms

Some dogs also face another unpleasant parasite commonly called "worms". These relentless organisms grow, feed, and take shelter within your dog's gastrointestinal system. Checking your dog's stool regularly may help identify the presence of some types of worms (roundworms and tapeworms, for example), but others (such as whipworms and hookworms) can be much less conspicuous. Signs indicating the presence of worms include excessive licking of the anal region or a persistent dragging of the rear end.

Since worms are parasites capable of spreading to human family members, an ounce of prevention may be worth even more than the proverbial pound of cure in their case. Keeping your yard free of your dog's feces is an excellent way to lower his risk of suffering from most kinds of worms. The soil contamination caused by excrement provides ideal conditions for many of these worms. It is also a wise idea to bring along a stool sample every time you visit the vet—what isn't visible to your naked eye will likely be much clearer under a microscope.

Preventive medications can protect your English Cocker from many of the illnesses caused by external parasites.

If your dog is diagnosed with worms, follow the instructions of your veterinarian carefully. Most importantly, never give your dog a *wormer* (a common name for the medication intended to rid a dog's body of worms) without your vet's knowledge and approval. If treatment is recommended, however, don't forget to ask your vet about how to treat your dog's environment as well, to prevent further infestation.

How to Remove a Flea or Tick

If you are lucky enough to detect fleas before they have had time to reproduce, use a fine-tooth comb to remove them and drop them into soapy water immediately. You may need to treat both your dog and your home if the problem persists.

Ticks can be a bit trickier to remove, but don't despair—and more importantly, don't panic. If you find a tick on your English Cocker Spaniel, use a pair of tweezers to carefully remove it. Since it is vital that you get both the tick's head and body out, your first objective will be getting the tick to simply let go on its own. To do this, use a pair of sterilized tweezers to grasp the tick's body and begin pulling it away from your dog's skin very gently. Apply steady pressure, but be sure not to squeeze too tightly. Jiggling the tick a bit is fine, but don't rotate it, as you don't want to separate the head from the body. If this happens, contact your veterinarian for further instruction.

Some vets suggest using a drop or two of isopropyl alcohol to get a tick to release a stubborn grip, but according to the American Lyme Disease Foundation, this method can backfire and even increase the chances of disease transmission. Once the tick is out, this is the time for the alcohol—drop the tick in some to kill it. (Never use your bare hands or feet to kill a tick.) As soon as the tick has been properly disposed of, clean the bite wound with disinfectant, and sterilize your tweezers with some fresh alcohol.

COMPLEMENTARY MEDICINE

Like alternative medicine for humans, alternative veterinary therapies have evolved into what is now often referred to as "complementary medicine", since these ancient healing techniques are being utilized more and more alongside more conventional forms of treatment. A dog suffering from epilepsy, for example, may initially need an anticonvulsant drug to help control seizures, but receiving regular acupuncture can lower the frequency of these episodes to the point at which only a lower dosage may be necessary—or to a point at which medication is no longer required at all.

Derived from the word "whole", the term "holistic medicine" refers to a group of independent techniques that share a common goal: to treat the mind, body, and spirit of the animal in crisis. Complementary therapies include such methods as acupuncture, acupressure, chiropractic care, homeopathy, and botanical medicine. Even our modern modality of physical therapy is based on some of the ancient techniques offered by holistic medicine.

Acupuncture

When I tell people I once took one of my Cocker Spaniels for Chinese acupuncture treatments, I usually get one of two reactions. About half the people ask me if I'm joking, and the other half want to know if the process was painful. The answer to both questions is a resounding no. While acupuncture carries an understandable connotation because of its most basic tenet—the insertion of needles into the body to alleviate pain or disease—the actual process is amazingly painless for the patient.

Even a dog with an excitable personality can benefit from this powerful technique; I should know, as my own dog definitely fits this description. When I brought Jonathan for his very first acupuncture treatment, I was more than a little skeptical myself—not so much about the efficacy of the technique, but about whether my dog would be able to tolerate it. Johnny was, well, there's no nice way to say it—a baby. (He cried so much during his first set of puppy shots that the vet didn't even charge me for the visit!) He also loved the attention he got from the adoring staff at our veterinary office and tended to be in "hyper mode" whenever we visited the hospital. How would the vet be able to keep him calm and still enough to insert the needles, I wondered?

My fears were put to rest within just minutes of arriving at our first appointment. Our vet began the acupuncture process by inserting a single needle into the back of Jonathan's head. This, as she explained to me, is a spot associated with calmness, and that is exactly what this step accomplished. By the time the remaining needles were in place, Johnny was resting comfortably on his side,

A heartworm preventive protects your dog from hookworms, roundworms, and other intestinal parasites as well as heartworm.

Don't Assume It's Worms

If your dog seems to be dragging his rear end along the floor or ground, do not automatically assume that your dog has worms. The problem may be impacted anal glands, an uncomfortable condition that is easily remedied. Your vet will be able to tell the difference between the two problems. If these glands (or sacs) that are situated on either side of your dog's anal opening do not empty regularly on their own, they often need the assistance of a veterinarian. Although this can be a rather unpleasant job because of the odor, some groomers also offer this service. If left engorged, impacted glands can become infected or even rupture.

as if he had decided to just lie back and relax for a while.

If you have never witnessed an acupuncture treatment, you may be surprised to learn that the needles are extremely tiny. I think many of us with phobias about such things automatically assume that a needle must always be large and foreboding. This is not the case with acupuncture at all. The needles our vet used were extremely thin and very flexible—hairlike would probably describe them best. Jonathan barely noticed as our vet inserted them into various spots surrounding the problem area of his left hind knee. After the needles were all in place, our vet used a mild form of incense that resembled a short cigar to heat up the needles. She told us this helped to stimulate the healing process.

If you are interested in utilizing acupuncture for your dog, a good place to begin is the American Academy of Veterinary Acupuncture (AAVA). Although many veterinary acupuncturists are also doctors of veterinary medicine, a very small number of vets are also certified acupuncturists. The ABVA can point you toward a licensed practitioner in your area. You should interview this person with the same scrutiny as you would a potential veterinarian.

Chiropractic Care

Chiropractic care is another form of medicine that often draws the disdain of skeptics, but like other forms of complementary medicine, it often provides legitimate relief from many canine health problems. Focusing on the spine and joints, a veterinary chiropractor does not diagnose disease, but rather treats symptoms directly. Chiropractic care literally addresses vertebral subluxations—dislocations of the bones or joints surrounding the spinal column that may be hindering the animal's health.

A chiropractor may be able to help if your dog suffers from lameness, seizures, or other chronic health problems. Your conventional veterinarian may also refer you to a chiropractor if your dog experiences an injury requiring this kind of expertise. Joint dysfunction can have a number of surprising causes—the wrong collar or harness, for example. A chiropractic exam can often help identify not only the solution to a problem, but also its most likely origin, thus helping you to prevent the problem from recurring.

Herbal Medicine

Dietary supplements and botanical medicine (also called herbal medicine) are other up and coming therapies in the veterinary community. From glucosamine and chondroitin to spirulina and wheat grass, plenty of natural remedies are out there for the open-minded dog owner. You must use both caution and common sense, however, when deciding which ones might be beneficial to your English Cocker Spaniel. Although most are indeed natural, this does not mean they cannot harm your dog. Ask your vet before adding any supplement (natural or otherwise) to your dog's regimen, but do consider trying one if she thinks that it might help with a specific problem your dog is facing.

Homeopathy

Some people might confuse the use of herbs with a very different modality called homeopathic medicine. Based on a very similar principle to the vaccination process, homeopathic medicine works by implementing infinitesimal doses of the substances that actually cause the disease a caregiver wishes to cure. While the amounts of the substances used in homeopathy are far removed from that of a vaccination, the premise of homeopathy is that the more these substances are diluted, the more powerful the effect on the patient will be.

When treated with homeopathic medicine, a dog may actually exhibit an intensification of symptoms before improvement begins. A dog with a fever, for example, may at first experience an even higher temperature. The ultimate goal, however, is a complete removal of all symptoms by creating a natural resistance to the illness.

Homeopathy is not something in which dog owners should dabble. Although it may be tempting to apply any knowledge you may already have in this area to your dog's current condition, it is always best to seek the advice of a trained professional, preferably a licensed veterinarian who is also skilled in this particular branch of medicine. Since the process involves such precise dosages, a high level of vigilance during treatment is mandatory.

Physical Therapy

The field of physical therapy is one of the most expanding professions within the human medical care community. People rely on this productive resource for help with all kinds of physical issues, ranging from hip fracture to strokes. It makes sense that canine patients suffering from similar problems can benefit from the canine version of this effective treatment. With the aid of such technological tools as ultrasound and electrical stimulation, canine physical therapists often start where conventional veterinarians leave off—after surgical procedures, during the healing of an injury to increase range of motion and overall strength, and even as a means of reducing pain and stiffness associated with a variety of chronic conditions. Canine physical therapists also utilize more traditional modalities such as massage, hydrotherapy (water), and therapeutic exercise. The exact combination of treatments depends on your dog's individual needs.

Any veterinarian can legally perform canine physical therapy, but it is important to note that very few vets receive training in this area as part of their formal education. Ideally, I recommend looking for a veterinarian who is also a licensed physical therapist. If you have trouble finding one of these dually trained individuals, however, expand your search to find both a veterinarian and licensed physical therapist who are willing to work together for the betterment of your English Cocker Spaniel's health.

Canine massage, although a component of many different complementary approaches, is a wondrous technique in its own right. On a more basic level, dog owners can even perform it at home for the mere pleasure it provides their pets. With just a small amount of instruction, you can simultaneously ease any tension your dog may be feeling and also offer your canine companion several health benefits, including increased circulation, relaxation of muscle spasms, and even lowered blood pressure. Think of how good a back rub feels to us; of course our dogs enjoy this simple indulgence, too.

Never perform canine massage or any other kind of complementary medicine without proper instruction from a qualified provider. Also, remember that no procedure should ever be used as a substitute for licensed veterinary care. Many good books and videos are available about the use of canine massage in the home. Your dog's individual reaction is paramount; listen to him and let him be your guide. You may be doing everything by the book, but if your dog shows any signs of displeasure, stop the massage immediately. Most dogs enjoy being massaged, but just like people, our dogs have a way of letting us know when something isn't right for them.

Also, remember that complementary therapies, like conventional medicine, are not an exact science. There is no way to know for certain which method will best serve your English Cocker Spaniel's needs. Sometimes results take time, but if something doesn't feel right, perhaps this particular method isn't the best one for your dog's problem. The very basis of the holistic approach is treating the whole being. Beware of any caregiver who doesn't take the time and effort to evaluate your dog completely. These few undesirable individuals can give the world of complementary medicine a bad name, but when used correctly, this diverse resource can offer your pet many worthwhile options for improved health and well being.

EMERGENCY HEALTH CARE

Few things are as nerve-wracking as being in the middle of a medical emergency. Unlike routine trips to the vet, in which we take step-by-step action to prevent conditions we can anticipate (like rabies or worms), crisis situations call for both immediate

Your dog may benefit from a combination of alternative therapies and conventional medicine.

Glucosamine

When our Cocker Spaniel, Jonathan, injured his leg, our vet suggested we begin giving him a glucosamine supplement with his meals. The objective was to lessen the effects that arthritis would likely have with such an injury. When Jonathan tore the ligament, scar tissue began forming as soon as the healing process began, and with this came the likelihood of arthritis. Combined with the acupuncture treatments, we saw dramatic results from the use of this supplement.

action and sound judgment—a challenging combination for many caring dog owners. Remaining calm, however difficult it may be, is the most important thing to remember in a medical emergency with your English Cocker Spaniel.

Dogs are very intuitive animals. They often know exactly how their owners are feeling without a word ever being said; emergencies are no exception. You wouldn't want your own anxiety to cause your dog additional stress and fear. You also wouldn't want to make your dog's situation worse by acting hastily. If your English Cocker has been hurt, bring him to the closest veterinarian immediately. If at all possible, phone ahead to let the office know you are coming. The staff may be able to provide you with important instructions that can help improve your dog's situation, and perhaps even save his life.

There are also a number of things you can do right now, so you will be prepared in the event of a particular kind of crisis down the road. In this sense, you can indeed anticipate emergencies and put the odds in your dog's favor.

The second most important thing to remember in the event of an emergency is that, medically speaking, dogs differ from their human counterparts dramatically. For example, while they are perfectly safe for most people, drugs like acetaminophen and ibuprofen can be deadly for an English Cocker. Of the human medications that *can* be used safely on our pets, most drugs require a drastic change in dosage when administered to dogs—and the amounts can vary from breed to breed or even between English Cocker Spaniels of different sizes. Never give your pet any medication without first checking with a veterinarian. Life-saving procedures like the Heimlich maneuver must also be executed very differently on a dog than on an adult human being.

Canine CPR

Cardiopulmonary resuscitation (CPR) is a combination of rescue breathing and chest compressions delivered to victims of cardiac arrest. Like the human form of this technique, canine CPR can be an invaluable resource when performed correctly, but the worst time to learn how to perform it is when it is necessary. The Humane Society of the United States and the American Red Cross have worked together to produce a first-aid manual for pet owners, including detailed instructions on canine CPR called *Pet First Aid* by

Bobbie Mammato, DVM, MPH, and Susie Duckworth. This guide, available throughout the UK as well, is an excellent foundation for creating your own canine first aid kit. You can also ask your veterinarian if any organizations in your area offer courses in canine CPR. If your English Cocker Spaniel has stopped breathing, and you do not know how to perform canine CPR, bring the dog to a veterinarian at once.

Choking

Like breathing difficulties, choking is a situation that demands immediate action. In some cases there may be no question as to what your dog has swallowed, but in others the cause might not be so obvious. Signs of choking include drooling, gagging, struggling to breathe, pawing at the face, and regurgitation.

If you haven't already, remove your dog's collar, and look into your dog's mouth. Although it may be tempting, resist the urge to place your hand inside your dog's mouth and pull at any object you may feel in his throat. Dogs have small bones that support the base of their tongues, and these can easily be mistaken for foreign objects. If you cannot identify or locate the item in question, lift your dog with his head pointing downward, as this may help to dislodge the object.

If this doesn't work, perform a modified Heimlich maneuver. Holding the dog around his waist so his bottom is closest to you, place a fist just behind the ribs. Compress the abdomen several times (begin with three) with quick upward pressure, and again check the mouth. Even if you are able to dislodge the object and your dog appears fine, it is a good idea to see your veterinarian immediately in case of any internal injury. Choking is considered a veterinary emergency. Whenever possible, try all of these methods while a friend or relative drives you and your dog to the nearest veterinary hospital.

Cuts

It is no secret that most English Cocker Spaniels love the outdoors. Unfortunately, many dangers lurk outside your home's four walls, just waiting for your dog to unknowingly step on them. As a result, lacerations are among the most prevalent canine injuries.

The first thing to do whenever your dog suffers a cut is try to stop the bleeding—ideally by applying pressure with a gauze pad soaked in cold water. Avoid using absorbent cotton, since it tends to stick to wounds and leave behind fibers. Once the bleeding has stopped, contact your veterinarian. If blood spurts from your dog's wound, immediate veterinary attention should be sought, as it is likely that an artery has been severed.

Apply firm pressure over the gauze pad until the bleeding subsides. Silver nitrate sticks or styptic powder are both helpful in speeding the clotting process. Remember to flush the cut with cleaning solution, saline, or plain water before covering it to prevent any debris from contaminating the wound. Once the bleeding has stopped and the area has been cleaned, cover the wound with a nonstick pad and secure it with a bandage.

TTouch

The Tellington TTouch is a popular form of animal massage therapy. This technique, created by an American named Linda Tellington-Jones in 1978, utilizes various types of touches, lifts, and movement exercise to help correct behavior problems (such as aggression and chewing), improve quality of life for aging pets, and even help with carsickness. It is now used throughout the world.

Eye Injuries

Since English Cockers are prone to eye problems, it is especially important that you bring your dog to the nearest veterinarian as soon as possible should an eye injury occur. Just like a human, a dog's initial reaction to a wound in this most delicate area will be to keep the eye closed as tightly as possible, so it is unlikely that you will be able to do anything to help your dog yourself. If you can indeed see that your English Cocker has something stuck inside the eye, you may try flushing the area with irrigation fluid or saline, but still get to the vet immediately thereafter. Your vet will need to examine the dog to determine if the cornea has been scratched. If a chemical irritant has entered the eye, flushing immediately is a must before promptly continuing to the vet's office. If both eyes appear injured, the problem is likely a chemical irritant.

Fighting Tooth and Nail

Bites from other animals—wild or otherwise—present a special cause for concern. Not only can bites inflict serious damage, but they also open the door for a number of serious bacterial infections and deadly viruses, such as rabies. Obviously, these risks are greatest when a wild or stray animal is involved, but it is vital that you bring your English Cocker Spaniel for a prompt veterinary examination even if the perpetrator is the dog next door. No matter how much your neighbor may assure you that her dog has been properly vaccinated, your dog should still be seen by a veterinarian as soon as possible to ensure the best possible outcome.

If a wild animal (such as a skunk or raccoon) bites your English Cocker, it will be necessary to booster his rabies vaccine. This potentially fatal virus can infect any warm-blooded animal, including humans, so be especially careful if you encounter the creature yourself. Since an animal can be rabid without showing any signs whatsoever, prompt veterinary attention is vital.

Skunked

The story of the dog that got too close to a skunk is a funny one until you are the one desperately bathing your pungent pup in one old wives' tale after another to no avail. Alas, tomato juice is not the panacea we all once believed, but don't despair; there is a remedy that works. If a skunk sprays your dog, be grateful that he wasn't bitten (make sure he indeed wasn't), hold your nose, and grab your dishwashing liquid.

A 3-quart mixture of hydrogen peroxide, 1/4 cup of baking soda, and just a teaspoon of the sudsy stuff will provide the best results for eliminating long-lasting odor. Wet your dog before applying the solution, and be sure to keep it away from your English Cocker's eyes, nose, and mouth. The mixture will fizz, so it is probably best to apply this treatment either in the tub or outdoors. *This fizz can create pressure and even explode if enclosed in a sealed container, so discard any unused portion of the treatment.* Also, remember to wear rubber gloves, or you will be sure to absorb at least some of the resilient odor during the de-skunking process.

While even you yourself may be tempted to giggle over your English Cocker's predicament, make sure you take the time to examine your pet carefully directly after the attack. If your dog's eyes are red and watery, chances are good that your English Cocker was sprayed in the face. This will not cause any permanent damage, but the results can be painful and may even result in temporary blindness. Your

Remaining calm is one of the most important things you can do in the event of a medical emergency with your English Cocker.

veterinarian may be able to suggest something to ease your dog's discomfort.

Heatstroke and Dehydration

I always try to bring along fresh water whenever I take my dogs anywhere. Even if we are just going for a quick drive, between the thrill of getting to go for a ride and the extra warm temperatures of the car before the air conditioning gets going, they both always seem to be thirsty before I reach my first stoplight. It is important to bear in mind, though, that dogs can become dehydrated right in their own homes—even in the middle of winter or on a rainy day. Keeping your dog indoors whenever the weather report warns that it may be dangerously hot for people to be outside is a great start, but you must always be sure your dog has access to fresh drinking water.

Whenever you see your English Cocker Spaniel's tongue hanging out of his mouth, it is a sure sign that he could use a drink. Since dogs lack sweat glands, they cannot release the excess heat in their bodies the way we do; instead they pant. Another indication that it might be time to refill your dog's water dish is if you yourself are feeling overly warm and thirsty. If you are spending time together outdoors, bring along enough water for

Cuts and lacerations are among the most common canine injuries. Dogs who spend a lot of time outside are especially prone to this ailment.

both of you, and don't forget a bowl for your furry friend. My mother purchased a special thermos for her Cocker Spaniel for this reason, but you can also find collapsible bowls in most pet stores. I keep one inside a bin in the trunk of my car along with other commonly used items, such as a blanket, first-aid kit, and wet wipes.

Signs of heatstroke include excessive panting, drooling, vomiting (with or without diarrhea), intensely red gums, and lethargy. If you suspect that your English Cocker is suffering from heatstroke, place him gently in a tub of cool (*not* cold) water and gently wrap a towel around him that has also been saturated with cool water. The goal here is to lower your dog's body temperature to 103°F (39°C). Use a rectal thermometer for

Your English Cocker's First-Aid Kit

Always keep the following items on hand in the event of a medical emergency:

- Antibiotic ointment
- Canine first-aid manual
- Children's diphenhydramine (antihistamine)
- Corn syrup
- Cotton swabs
- Emergency phone numbers (including poison control, emergency veterinarian, and your dog's regular vet)
- Flashlight
- Hydrogen peroxide
- Instant ice pack
- Ipecac syrup
- Liquid bandages
- Mineral oil
- Nonstick gauze pads, gauze, and tape
- Oral syringe or eyedropper
- Rectal thermometer
- Saline solution
- Scissors
- Silver nitrate stick
- Soap
- Styptic powder or pencil
- Tweezers
- Any other item your veterinarian recommends keeping on hand

You may also want to assemble a portable emergency kit for your dog if you spend a lot of time hiking, camping, or traveling together. With either type of kit, remember to keep an eye on expiration dates and toss any products before they should no longer be used.

the most accurate reading, and then bring him to the veterinary hospital immediately after this goal has been accomplished.

Poison

When a previously healthy dog suddenly becomes ill for no apparent reason, the cause is often poisoning. Although many of us think of a few well-known items as being poisonous to dogs—

chocolate and onions, for example—these are hardly the only substances that threaten our pets' health. A toxin also does not have to be swallowed for it to be a threat. Many dangerous chemicals can wreak havoc on our dogs' systems after being inhaled or absorbed by the skin, as well. Sometimes owners might not even be aware that a poisoning has occurred.

Common signs of poisoning include vomiting, diarrhea, and trembling; but many chemical toxins do not trigger distinctive signs of illness. This can make identification of the toxin nearly impossible in many cases. If you suspect that your dog has been exposed to any form of poison, seek advice from a qualified professional immediately.

Ipecac syrup readily induces vomiting, but this approach can prove to be counterproductive. Caustic toxins, such as drain cleaner, can burn the throat a second time when brought back up through the esophagus. If there is any question as to what substance your dog has ingested, wait for instructions from a veterinarian before taking any action.

Always make sure your dog has access to fresh water, especially when outdoors in warm weather.

The ASPCA Animal Poison Control Center offers an emergency hotline at 1-888-426-4435. You can call from anywhere in the world, anytime, 24 hours a day, 365 days a year. (There is a charge of $55 USD per case.) You will be asked the name and amount of the toxin your dog was exposed to, the length of time that has passed; the breed, age, sex, and weight of your dog; and the symptoms he is displaying. You will also need to provide your name, address, telephone number, and credit card information.

Trauma

Trauma is a blanket term for severe injury or shock that usually results from a serious fall or other accident. A dog who has experienced any kind of trauma needs immediate veterinary treatment, but great care needs to be employed when transporting the animal. First, it is imperative to remember that a dog in the midst of trauma may not react to those around him as he normally would. Many aren't even able to recognize their concerned owners. For this important reason, refrain from getting too close to the dog's face. Second, there may be a very specific way in which you should move the dog, so whenever possible, contact the veterinary hospital before doing anything at all.

If your dog is bleeding, a rubber band can serve as a makeshift tourniquet. If any limbs appear to be broken or distorted, use extra care not to handle them when moving him. A stiff surface, such as an ordinary board, can make a great impromptu stretcher; a blanket or a coat will suffice if nothing else is available. If you are alone and cannot hold the dog in place, use a belt or rope to secure him for the ride to the veterinary hospital. Use rolled towels or another coat to keep him warm and prevent him from moving around. Keeping your dog as still as possible can prevent further injury from occurring on your way to the vet's office.

SENIOR CARE

Although the old ratio of one dog year being equivalent to seven human years is now said to be unreliable, it still seems terribly unfair that our canine companions age so much more rapidly than we do. I have often wished that dogs could have a lifespan more comparable to parrots or elephants or turtles, some of which can rival our own. Unfortunately, the only thing we can do to hinder the signs of the aging process in our English Cocker Spaniels is provide them with the best possible preventive care. This includes taking them for regular visits to the veterinarian, feeding them healthy diets free of byproducts, and keeping them safely on a leash whenever we venture out into the great wide open with our truest of friends.

Even with the best of care, our English Cocker Spaniels must usually face a number of unpleasant effects from the aging process. You may need to be extra careful when grooming if your dog develops the usual lumps and bumps of old age. Most of these will be benign, but always check with your veterinarian. As in my case, it just may end up providing you with precious extra time together if the lump is malignant and should be removed.

Many signs of aging are purely aesthetic, but others can interfere with your dog's everyday life. Just because these issues are normal does not mean that you cannot do anything about them, though.

English Cockers in Cars

The most frequent cause of canine heatstroke is owners leaving their dogs in cars. One might suppose this is only a danger during warmer weather, but more than a few dogs have succumbed to this dangerous condition while left in their owners' vehicles in the middle of winter with the heater running. A hot car can reach temperatures high enough to kill a dog in just minutes. Leaving a window open is not enough; your dog can still become overheated. For your English Cocker Spaniel's safety, never leave him unattended in your car — ever.

As dogs get older, they naturally show some signs of aging, such as weakened senses and reduced energy level.

Arthritis, for example, is a very treatable affliction. Slower movement is one of the most blatant signs of the disease; if your dog appears to be suffering, contact your veterinarian to discuss what can be done to help him. You can also take steps at home to accommodate your English Cocker's specific needs. Dog beds made with orthopedic foam and even heated beds are available for seniors with arthritis or other joint problems.

Not only is your elderly dog more vulnerable to falls, but also the risks associated with such accidents are greater now. Especially if your dog's eyesight has diminished, consider placing a baby gate in front of any stairways within your home. Additionally, be sure to turn on lights whenever your dog does climb or go down stairs at night.

As your English Cocker enters his senior years—around the age of 9 or 10—you may also want to increase the frequency of his routine veterinary visits from once to twice each year. By having your veterinarian examine your dog more often, you will be better able to identify issues before they become bigger problems. This can be vital in helping your elderly dog overcome these obstacles.

THE END OF AN ERA

When I lost my first Cocker Spaniel, my veterinarian sent me a sympathy card with a hand-written note saying that it was the end of era. At this bleak time, I had received many such cards, but my vet's words struck me in a way few others did. It *was* the end of an era—the end of a lifetime for my dog, and also in a way, for me. Our pets are such huge parts of our lives that when they die, it feels like a part of us dies with them.

No matter how much time we have with them, it never seems quite enough. Not only do we feel sad at their passing, but in many cases we also feel cheated. We are left with an overwhelming feeling that life isn't fair, and in some cases with a determined resistance toward opening our hearts again. Just like love itself, grief has a way of making us believe that no one else has ever experienced these feelings. It can be devastatingly lonely, even if we are lucky enough to have many friends and family members there to help us through it all.

There is no single right way to deal with grief. Perhaps this is part of what makes it so difficult. There are, however, many wonderful resources out there for people in need of talking about their loss. Grieving your beloved English Cocker Spaniel is necessary—there is no way around it but through it. Sharing your feelings about the experience may at least make it slightly more bearable. You will also very likely be helping someone else in this position in the process.

Helping Children Cope With the Loss

Parents especially need to make communication a priority. Losing a pet is usually the first death a child must experience. It is very common for children to blame themselves, their parents, or the veterinarian for not doing enough to save their pet's life. They may also fear the loss of another family member. Telling your children how you are feeling can help them better understand their own emotions surrounding the death of their pet. Be honest with them, even if you are tempted to try to shield them from the experience. Some parents will tell a child that a dog ran away or went to live with someone else to spare them the sadness, but ultimately the loss will still exist. By being straightforward in acknowledging your own sadness, you will teach your child that it is okay to feel sad and frustrated over this very difficult part of life.

Other animals within your home may also grieve the loss. Acting lethargic, refusing to eat or drink, and even vocalizing excessively are all common signs that your other dog is missing his housemate. For this reason, it is just as important for your living dog as it is for you to maintain your normal routine. It will be very different going for walks with just the two of you if your deceased English Cocker always used to join you, but you must take this initiative. Your other pets are depending on you to lovingly help them through this.

If you have no other pets that need your care, the grieving process can be even more difficult, especially if you live alone. Talk to your friends, family, and neighbors, and get out of the house

Aging Gracefully

I once saw a t-shirt that read "Getting older isn't for cry-babies." At the time, I was immediately reminded of my then 10-year-old Cocker Spaniel who had successfully battled cancer, couldn't hear nearly as well as he once did, and sported his own unique mix of warts and gray hairs—all signs that he was no longer the youthful pup that I still oddly considered him to be. Jonathan was indeed no cry-baby. He never groaned when he got up from a nap, even though I know his arthritis sometimes made it a difficult task. Instead, he continued to follow me up and down the stairs each and every time I went one way or another throughout the house. He still showered me with the same enthusiastic greeting every time I returned home, whether I'd been gone two minutes or two hours. I remember wishing he could tell me his secret, because that was the kind of senior citizen I wished I could be someday.

How Can I Cope With My Grief?

While grief is a personal experience, you need not face loss alone. Many forms of support are available, including pet bereavement counseling services, pet-loss support hotlines, local or online Internet bereavement groups, books, videos, and magazine articles. Here are a few suggestions to help you cope:

- Acknowledge your grief and give yourself permission to express it.
- Don't hesitate to reach out to others who can lend a sympathetic ear.
- Write about your feelings, either in a journal or a poem.
- Call your local humane society to see whether it offers a pet-loss support group or can refer you to one. You may also want to ask your veterinarian or local animal shelter about available pet-loss hotlines.
- Explore the Internet for pet-loss support groups and coping information.
- Prepare a memorial for your pet.

(Courtesy of the HSUS)

as often as possible. Take part in community activities, and when you are feeling up to it, consider spending some time volunteering for your local animal shelter. One of the best ways to honor the memory of your English Cocker Spaniel is by helping other animals.

If you know someone who has recently lost a pet, make an effort to let her know you care. If you have been through this kind of loss yourself, share your feelings about your own experience— particularly anything that helped you get through it. Getting your friend involved in a favorite activity can also be helpful, even if at first you are met with resistance.

One thing you should never do, however, is get your grieving friend a new dog. While your friend may one day, someday soon even, decide that she is ready for a new pet, pets should never be given as gifts. Many owners find that once they have finished grieving they indeed have enough room in their heart for another dog, but this is a deeply personal decision. A new dog also comes with a great amount of responsibility, and the decision to take that on should rest solely with the owner.

When You're Ready to Love Another

There is nothing like the love and companionship of a dog. Most English Cocker Spaniel owners can hardly imagine their lives without their favorite breed, but for many who have recently lost their dear canine friends, waiting a while to get another dog seems the only right thing to do. To give themselves sufficient time to grieve and out of respect for their deceased English Cocker, these people need to wait. Others, in contrast, feel they can grieve their loss while also bringing a new dog into their lives. Is there anything wrong with either perspective? Absolutely not. We all must do what works best for us individually.

If you have suffered the loss of your English Cocker Spaniel and are now ready to welcome another English Cocker (or other breed) into your home, the most important thing is making sure you take enough time to find the right dog for you and your family. Take all the steps that you would do if you were looking for your very first dog—re-read the sections in this book about selecting a breeder, ask numerous questions when visiting kennels, and most importantly, wait to make a decision until everything feels right.

When (or whether) to acquire a new pet after the loss of your dog is a personal decision—you will know when you're ready to welcome another dog into your life.

Please don't dismiss the animals available through your local humane society or English Cocker rescue group. These organizations can help match you with a wonderful dog in desperate need of a new home. Whether you want an energetic youngster or an older, more subdued dog, adoption can be an invaluable resource for all involved.

Above all, remember that love never dies. I believe we are all better for the love of our dear pets, both past and present. You can never replace the dog you have lost, but you just may find a new canine friend that needs you as much as you need the love of a dog in your life.

RESOURCES

ASSOCIATIONS AND ORGANIZATIONS

BREED CLUBS

American Kennel Club (AKC)
5580 Centerview Drive
Raleigh, NC 27606
Telephone: (919) 233-9767
Fax: (919) 233-3627
E-mail: info@akc.org
www.akc.org

Canadian Kennel Club (CKC)
89 Skyway Avenue, Suite 100
Etobicoke, Ontario M9W 6R4
Telephone: (416) 675-5511
Fax: (416) 675-6506
E-mail: information@ckc.ca
www.ckc.ca

Federation Cynologique Internationale (FCI)
Secretariat General de la FCI
Place Albert 1er, 13
B – 6530 Thuin
Belqique
www.fci.be

The Kennel Club
1 Clarges Street
London
W1J 8AB
Telephone: 0870 606 6750
Fax: 0207 518 1058
www.the-kennel-club.org.uk

United Kennel Club (UKC)
100 E. Kilgore Road
Kalamazoo, MI 49002-5584
Telephone: (269) 343-9020
Fax: (269) 343-7037
E-mail: pbickell@ukcdogs.com
www.ukcdogs.com

RESCUE ORGANIZATIONS AND ANIMAL WELFARE GROUPS

American Humane Association (AHA)
63 Inverness Drive East
Englewood, CO 80112
Telephone: (303) 792-9900
Fax: 792-5333
www.americanhumane.org

American Society for the Prevention of Cruelty to Animals (ASPCA)
424 E. 92nd Street
New York, NY 10128-6804
Telephone: (212) 876-7700
www.aspca.org

Royal Society for the Prevention of Cruelty to Animals (RSPCA)
Telephone: 0870 3335 999
Fax: 0870 7530 284
www.rspca.org.uk

The Humane Society of the United States (HSUS)
2100 L Street, NW
Washington DC 20037
Telephone: (202) 452-1100
www.hsus.org

SPORTS

International Agility Link (IAL)
Global Administrator: Steve Drinkwater
E-mail: yunde@powerup.au
www.agilityclick.com/~ial

North American Dog Agility Council
11522 South Hwy 3
Cataldo, ID 83810
www.nadac.com

United States Dog Agility Association
P.O. Box 850955
Richardson, TX 75085-0955
Telephone: (972) 487-2200
www.usdaa.com

VETERINARY AND HEALTH RESOURCES

Academy of Veterinary Homeopathy (AVH)
P.O. Box 9280
Wilmington, DE 19809
Telephone: (866) 652-1590
Fax: (866) 652-1590
E-mail: office@TheAVH.org
www.theavh.org

American Academy of Veterinary Acupuncture (AAVA)
100 Roscommon Drive, Suite 320
Middletown, CT 06457
Telephone: (860) 635-6300
Fax: (860) 635-6400
E-mail: office@aava.org
www.aava.org

American Animal Hospital Association (AAHA)
P.O. Box 150899
Denver, CO 80215-0899
Telephone: (303) 986-2800
Fax: (303) 986-1700
E-mail: info@aahanet.org
www.aahanet.org/index.cfm

American College of Veterinary Internal Medicine (ACVIM)
1997 Wadsworth Blvd., Suite A
Lakewood, CO 80214-5293
Telephone: (800) 245-9081
Fax: (303) 231-0880
Email: ACVIM@ACVIM.org
www.acvim.org

American College of Veterinary Ophthalmologists (ACVO)
P.O. Box 1311
Meridian, Idaho 83860
Telephone: (208) 466-7624
Fax: (208) 466-7693
E-mail: office@acvo.com
www.acvo.com

American Heartworm Society
PO Box 667
Batavia, IL 60510
E-mail: heartwormsociety@earthlink.net
www.heartwormsociety.org

American Holistic Veterinary Medical Association (AHVMA)
2218 Old Emmorton Road
Bel Air, MD 21015
Telephone: (410) 569-0795
Fax: (410) 569-2346
E-mail: office@ahvma.org
www.ahvma.org

American Veterinary Chiropractic Association (AVCA)
442154 E 140 Rd.
Bluejacket, OK 74333
Telephone: (918) 784-2231
E-mail amvetchiro@aol.com
www.animalchiropractic.org

American Veterinary Medical Association (AVMA)
1931 North Meacham Road – Suite 100
Schaumburg, IL 60173
Telephone: (847) 925-8070
Fax: (847) 925-1329
E-mail: avmainfo@avma.org
www.avma.org

Animal Behavior Society
Indiana University
2611 East 10th Street #170
Bloomington IN 47408-2603
Telephone: (812) 856-5541
E-mail: aboffice@indiana.edu
www.animalbehavior.org

ASPCA Animal Poison Control Center
1717 South Philo Road, Suite 36
Urbana, IL 61802
Telephone: (888) 426-4435
www.aspca.org

British Veterinary Association (BVA)
7 Mansfield Street
London
W1G 9NQ
Telephone: 020 7636 6541
Fax: 020 7436 2970
E-mail: bvahq@bva.co.uk
www.bva.co.uk

Canine Eye Registration Foundation (CERF)
VMDB/CERF
1248 Lynn Hall
625 Harrison St.
Purdue University
West Lafayette, IN 47907-2026
Telephone: (765) 494-8179
E-mail: CERF@vmbd.org
www.vmdb.org

Orthopedic Foundation for Animals (OFA)
2300 NE Nifong Blvd
Columbus, Missouri 65201-3856
Telephone: (573) 442-0418
Fax: (573) 875-5073
Email: ofa@offa.org
www.offa.org

MISCELLANEOUS

American Boarding Kennels Association
4575 Galley Road
Suite 400A
Colorado Springs, CO 80915
Email: info@abka.com
www.abka.com

Association for Pet Loss and Bereavement, Inc. (APLB)
P.O. Box 106
Brooklyn, NY 11230
Telephone: (718) 382-0690
E-mail: aplb@aplb.org
www.aplb.org

Association of Pet Dog Trainers (APDT)
150 Executive Center Drive Box 35
Greenville, SC 29615
Telephone: (800) PET-DOGS
Fax: (864) 331-0767
E-mail: information@apdt.com
www.apdt.com

Delta Society
875 124th Ave NE, Suite 101
Bellevue, WA 98005
Telephone: (425) 226-7357
Fax: (425) 235-1076
E-mail: info@deltasociety.org
www.deltasociety.org

Dogs with Disabilities
1406 East Small Lane
Mount Prosepct, IL 60056
Telephone: (847) 296-8277

National Association of Dog Obedience Instructors
PMB 369
729 Grapevine Hwy.
Hurst, TX 76054-2085
www.nadoi.org

National Association of Professional Pet Sitters
15000 Commerce Parkway, Suite C
Mt. Laurel, New Jersey 08054
Telephone: (856) 439-0324
Fax: (856) 439-0525
E-mail: napps@ahint.com
www.petsitters.org

National Dog Groomers Association of America
P.O. Box 101
Clark, PA 16113
Telephone: (724) 962-2711
E-mail:ndga@nationaldoggromers.com
www.nationaldoggroomers.com

Pet Sitters International
201 East King Street
King, NC 27021-9161
Telephone: (336) 983-9222
Fax: (336) 983-5266
E-mail: info@petsit.com
www.petsit.com

Professional Handlers Association
17017 Norbrook Drive
Olney, MD 20832
Telephone: (301) 924-0089
www.phadoghandlers.com

Professional Pet Transports, Inc.
59154 Trafton Lane
John Day, OR 97845
Telephone: 1-866-ARE-PETS
(273-7387)
E-mail: questions@pro-pet-transports.com
www.pro-pet-transports.com

Therapy Dogs International (TDI)
88 Bartley Road
Flanders, NJ 07836
Telephone: (973) 252-9800
Fax: (973) 252-7171
E-mail: tdi@gti.net
www.tdi-dog.org

PUBLICATIONS
BOOKS

Becker, Susan Cope, *Deaf Dog: A Book of Advice, Facts and Experiences about Canine Deafness*, S.C. Becker

Levin, Caroline, *Living with a Blind Dog*, Lantern Publications

Mammato, Bobbie, and Susie Duckworth, *Pet First Aid,* American Red Cross

MAGAZINES

AKC *Family Dog*
American Kennel Club
260 Madison Avenue
New York, NY 10016
Telephone: (800) 490-5675
E-mail: familydog@akc.org
www.akc.org/pubs/familydog

AKC *Gazette*
American Kennel Club
260 Madison Avenue
New York, NY 10016
Telephone: (800) 533-7323
E-mail: gazette@akc.org
www.akc.org/pubs/gazette

Dog & Kennel
Pet Publishing, Inc.
7-L Dundas Circle
Greensboro, NC 27407
Telephone: (336) 292-4272
Fax: (336) 292-4272
E-mail: info@petpublishing.com
www.dogandkennel.com

Dog Fancy
Subscription Department
P.O. Box 53264
Boulder, CO 80322-3264
Telephone: (800) 365-4421
E-mail: barkback@dogfancy.com
www.dogfancy.com

DEDICATION

To Mary LaChance, whose knowledge of Cocker Spaniels is surpassed only by her love for this amazing breed and her generous spirit as both a teacher and a friend.

ACKNOWLEDGEMENTS

I would like to thank the following people for taking the time to speak with me about their precious Cocker Spaniels:

Norma Gassett, Patricia Faucher, K. Kelly, Denise Pratt, Stan Rawlinson, LeeAnne Roy, Kim Tees of Maine Cocker Rescue, Karen Schultz, Elaine Thomas, Andrea Vienneau, Jim Zimmerlin of Zim Family Cocker Spaniels

ABOUT THE AUTHOR

Tammy Gagne is a freelance writer who specializes in the health and behavior of companion animals. She is a regular contributor to several national pet care magazines and has owned purebred dogs for more than 25 years. In addition to being an avid dog lover, she is also an experienced aviculturist and writes a bi-monthly column that appears in *Bird Times* magazine. She resides in northern New England with her husband, son, Cocker Spaniels, and parrots.

PHOTO CREDITS

Utekhina Anna (Shutterstock): 27

emannuelle bonzani (Shutterstock): 13, 16, 38, 62, 159

Paul Cowen (Shutterstock): 25, 157

Interpet: 29, 56, 66, 77, 121

Eric Isselee (Shutterstock): 46, 68, 193

Pers-Anders Jansson (Shutterstock): 149, 201

MISHELLA (Shutterstock): 31

SueC (Shutterstock): 52, 128

Claudia Steininger (Shutterstock): 14

All other photos courtesy of Isabelle Francais

Front cover and back cover photos: Isabelle Francais

Nylabone® Cares.

Dogs of all ages, breeds, and sizes have enjoyed our world-famous chew bones for over 50 years. For the safest, healthiest, and happiest lifetime your dog can possibly have, choose from a variety of Nylabone® Pet Products!

Toys

Treats

Chews

Crates

Grooming